French P

Everything You Need to Know

Introduction: Discovering French Polynesia's Enchantment 6

A Brief Overview: Geography and Location of French Polynesia 8

Pre-European History: The Polynesians' Arrival and Settlements 10

Early European Contact: Tracing the Arrival of Explorers 12

Colonial Era: French Influence and Impact on the Islands 14

Path to Autonomy: French Polynesia's Political Evolution 16

Modern Governance: The Structure of the Territorial Government 18

Flora and Fauna: Exploring the Rich Wildlife of French Polynesia 20

Gastronomic Delights: Savory Cuisine of the Islands 22

Traditional Dishes: A Culinary Journey into Local Specialties 24

Tahitian Cuisine: The Signature Flavors of the Islands 26

Top Tourist Attractions: Must-Visit Gems of French Polynesia 28

Bora Bora: The Ultimate Island Paradise 30

Moorea: Enchanting Landscapes and Adventure 32

Tahiti: Heartbeat of French Polynesia 34

Raiatea and Taha'a: Historical and Sacred Wonders 36

Huahine: The Garden of Eden 38

Nuku Hiva and Hiva Oa: Marquesas Archipelago's Treasures 40

Rangiroa and Fakarava: Exploring the Tuamotus Atolls 42

Humpback Whales and Dolphins: Marveling at Marine Life 44

Coral Reefs: Diving into Colorful Underwater Worlds 46

Traditional Arts and Crafts: Experiencing Polynesian Creativity 48

Music and Dance: The Rhythms of Polynesian Culture 50

Taputapuātea: UNESCO World Heritage Site of Marae Complex 52

Heiva Festival: Celebrating Polynesian Culture 54

Tiki Culture: Unraveling Ancient Symbols and Meanings 56

Navigation and Wayfinding: Ancient Polynesian Skills 58

Languages of French Polynesia: Beyond French and Tahitian 60

Basic Tahitian Language: Useful Phrases for Travelers 62

Religion and Spirituality: Ancient and Modern Beliefs 64

Family and Community: Understanding Social Structure 66

Tāne Mahuta and Vātea: Gods and Mythology 68

Tattoos: Indelible Markers of Polynesian Identity 70

Pearl Farming: Exploring the Industry of Black Pearls 72

Copra Production: The Essence of Polynesian Economy 74

Impact of Tourism: Balancing Preservation and Development 76

Challenges of Climate Change: Protecting the Fragile Ecosystem 78

Art of Outrigger Canoeing: Traditional Sport and Recreation 80

Land and Water Sports: Thrilling Adventures for All 82

Island Hopping: Creating Your Ideal Itinerary 84

Planning Your Trip: Tips and Essentials for Travelers 86

Cultural Sensitivity: Respecting Local Traditions 89

French Polynesia's Future: Embracing Sustainability and Growth 92

Epilogue 95

Introduction: Discovering French Polynesia's Enchantment

Welcome to the enchanting world of French Polynesia, a mesmerizing collection of islands nestled in the vast expanse of the South Pacific Ocean. This tropical paradise is a captivating blend of breathtaking landscapes, vibrant cultures, and an unparalleled sense of tranquility that beckons travelers from all corners of the globe. From the moment you set foot on these idyllic shores, you'll be swept away by the allure of this remote and untouched haven.

French Polynesia is an overseas collectivity of France, composed of 118 islands and atolls scattered across five distinct archipelagos: Society Islands, Tuamotus, Marquesas Islands, Austral Islands, and Gambier Islands. Each archipelago boasts its unique character, offering an extraordinary diversity of experiences that make French Polynesia an unrivaled destination for every type of adventurer.

At the heart of this tropical paradise lies Tahiti, the largest and most famous of the Society Islands. Known as the "Queen of the Pacific," Tahiti serves as the cultural, political, and economic hub of French Polynesia. Here, you'll find a harmonious fusion of ancient Polynesian traditions and modern French influences, creating a cultural tapestry that's both captivating and inviting.

Stepping beyond the bustling urban centers of Tahiti, you'll encounter the pristine beauty of the other islands, each a masterpiece of nature's craftsmanship. Bora Bora, a jewel in the South Pacific crown, beckons with its iconic turquoise lagoon and towering emerald peaks. Moorea, Tahiti's sister island, lures visitors with its lush landscapes and abundance of outdoor adventures.

As you traverse the archipelagos, you'll discover that French Polynesia is a haven for marine life enthusiasts and divers alike. The coral reefs that embrace these islands are teeming with an astonishing array of colorful fish, rays, sharks, and playful dolphins. And during the whale-watching season, the waters come alive with the graceful dances of humpback whales, an awe-

—

6

inspiring spectacle that leaves a lasting impression on any lucky observer.

Beyond its natural wonders, French Polynesia boasts a rich tapestry of cultural heritage. The Polynesian people, renowned for their warm hospitality, proudly preserve their ancestral traditions through captivating music, dance, and mesmerizing ceremonies. The rhythmic beats of drums and the melodic ukulele tunes echo throughout the islands, creating an immersive experience into the heart of Polynesian life.

As you delve deeper into French Polynesia's enchantment, you'll encounter ancient marae, sacred sites where ancient rituals and ceremonies were once held, and where the spirits of ancestors still seem to linger. The intricate wood carvings and stone sculptures tell stories of a vibrant history that continues to shape the present.

French Polynesia's cuisine is a delectable fusion of traditional Polynesian flavors and French gastronomy. Savor the tantalizing aromas of fresh seafood, tropical fruits, and aromatic spices that grace the tables of local restaurants and bustling food markets. Each dish tells a tale of cultural heritage, with cooking techniques passed down through generations, ensuring that the flavors remain authentic and unforgettable.

Whether you seek the tranquility of secluded beaches, the thrill of water sports, the romance of an overwater bungalow, or the exploration of untouched nature, French Polynesia offers an abundance of experiences to cater to your every desire.

This book is your passport to uncovering the secrets of French Polynesia. In the chapters that follow, we will take you on a journey through the islands' history, wildlife, cuisine, important tourist sights, historic cities, and cultural treasures. Prepare to be immersed in the essence of paradise as we unveil the hidden gems and timeless allure of French Polynesia. So, grab your sun hat, pack your curiosity, and let's embark on this unforgettable adventure together. Let the enchantment begin!

A Brief Overview: Geography and Location of French Polynesia

Nestled like a scattering of emerald jewels in the vast expanse of the South Pacific Ocean lies the enchanting destination of French Polynesia. This overseas collectivity of France is a captivating archipelago composed of 118 islands and atolls, which are grouped into five distinct archipelagos: Society Islands, Tuamotus, Marquesas Islands, Austral Islands, and Gambier Islands.

The Society Islands, situated in the central part of French Polynesia, are arguably the most famous and alluring. Tahiti, the largest and most significant of all the islands, serves as the administrative and cultural center of French Polynesia. Its vibrant capital, Papeete, is the gateway for many travelers entering this tropical paradise.

Stretching out from Tahiti are the stunning sister islands of Moorea, with its dramatic peaks and lush valleys, and Bora Bora, often referred to as the "Pearl of the Pacific" for its picturesque lagoon and overwater bungalows that seem to float on the water's surface.

The Tuamotus, known as the "Dangerous Archipelago," are a vast collection of coral atolls renowned for their incredible marine biodiversity. These low-lying rings of coral and sand encircle azure lagoons, offering unparalleled opportunities for diving and snorkeling adventures.

In the remote Marquesas Islands, located to the northeast of the Society Islands, rugged volcanic landscapes captivate travelers with their dramatic beauty. The Marquesas boast a rich cultural heritage, celebrated through traditional arts, crafts, and ceremonies that have endured the test of time.

Further to the south are the Austral Islands, a group of five high islands and dozens of small islets. Known for their verdant landscapes and ancient volcanic activity, these islands offer an off-the-beaten-path escape for intrepid explorers seeking solitude and natural wonders.

The Gambier Islands, situated in the far southeast of French Polynesia, are characterized by their rocky terrain and deep blue lagoons. These remote islands are known for their distinctive black pearls, a prized gem that emerges from the depths of the sea.

French Polynesia's geography plays a crucial role in its unique climate, which can be divided into two distinct seasons: the dry season (April to October) and the wet season (November to March). The islands enjoy a warm tropical climate year-round, with average temperatures ranging from 70°F (21°C) in the cooler months to 86°F (30°C) during the warmer periods.

Due to its remote location, French Polynesia is one of the most isolated places on Earth. Its nearest neighbor is Pitcairn Island, located over a thousand miles away. The islands' isolation has contributed to the preservation of its unique flora and fauna, making it a haven for nature enthusiasts and researchers alike.

The archipelago's enchanting landscapes include towering volcanic peaks, lush rainforests, cascading waterfalls, and pristine beaches with powdery white sands. The coral reefs that encircle many of the islands teem with diverse marine life, making French Polynesia a paradise for snorkelers and scuba divers.

Pre-European History: The Polynesians' Arrival and Settlements

Long before the arrival of European explorers, the remote islands of French Polynesia were home to a remarkable group of people known as the Polynesians. These skilled navigators and seafarers are believed to have ventured across vast expanses of ocean to discover and settle the islands of the South Pacific, including what we now know as French Polynesia.

The Polynesians' journey to the islands is an extraordinary tale of courage, determination, and navigational prowess. They were part of the larger Austronesian-speaking population, who are thought to have originated from Taiwan and began their migration thousands of years ago. Through generations of exploration and voyaging, these early Polynesian seafarers gradually made their way southward, navigating by the stars, winds, and currents to reach new lands.

French Polynesia's settlement history is a testament to the incredible maritime skills of the Polynesians. Their remarkable double-hulled canoes, often called "wa'a" or "waka," were constructed using traditional methods and materials such as wood, coconut fibers, and plant resins. These sturdy vessels were crucial to their successful navigation across vast distances, allowing them to carry supplies and families to establish new homes on distant shores.

The exact timing of the Polynesians' arrival in French Polynesia is still a subject of ongoing research and debate among historians and archaeologists. However, evidence suggests that the islands were first settled around 200 AD, with successive waves of migration occurring over the centuries that followed.

The islands of French Polynesia offered abundant resources for sustenance and livelihoods. The Polynesians adapted their agricultural practices to suit the diverse environments of the islands, cultivating taro, sweet potatoes, yams, breadfruit, and other crops that thrived in the fertile volcanic soils. They also domesticated animals such as pigs and chickens, which became integral to their daily lives.

One of the most remarkable aspects of the Polynesian settlement is the way they spread across such vast distances, creating a network of communities and cultural exchange. Despite the remote locations of the islands, there was a remarkable sense of connectedness among the Polynesian people, evident in the similarities of their language, customs, and religious beliefs.

The oral traditions and legends passed down through generations offer insights into their ancestral journeys and the significant role of celestial navigation in their expeditions. The navigational techniques were highly guarded and transmitted orally from master navigator to apprentice, ensuring the continuity of this crucial knowledge.

As the Polynesian settlements flourished, distinct island cultures began to develop, each adapting to its unique environment and resources. The islands' volcanic topography and isolation led to the evolution of distinct societies, with variations in art, architecture, social structures, and religious practices.

The islands' abundant marine resources played a central role in the Polynesians' lives. Fishing became a vital part of their subsistence, and they developed intricate fish-catching techniques using nets, traps, and spears. Additionally, they were skilled sailors and fishers, venturing far out to sea in their canoes to catch large ocean fish like tuna and marlin.

The ancient Polynesian societies were organized into chiefdoms, led by powerful chiefs and noble families. The chiefs held significant authority, and their lineages were often traced back to legendary figures and gods, creating a strong connection between the spiritual and political realms.

Through their mastery of the ocean, the Polynesians established a thriving trade network, exchanging goods and cultural practices among the islands. This interconnectedness enriched their societies with new ideas, technologies, and artistic expressions, further shaping the unique cultural tapestry of French Polynesia.

Early European Contact: Tracing the Arrival of Explorers

The pristine and remote islands of French Polynesia, which had been home to the indigenous Polynesians for centuries, first came into contact with European explorers in the late 16th century. The discovery and subsequent exploration of these South Pacific islands were part of the larger Age of Exploration, during which European powers sought to expand their territories and trade routes across the globe.

The first European to set eyes on French Polynesia was the Spanish explorer Álvaro de Mendaña de Neira. In 1595, Mendaña embarked on a voyage in search of the fabled Southern Continent, which was believed to exist in the South Pacific. During his expedition, he sighted the Marquesas Islands, but due to navigational challenges and unfavorable winds, he was unable to make a successful landing. Disheartened, Mendaña continued his exploration eastward, leaving the islands undiscovered by European powers for several more decades.

In the early 18th century, another European explorer, the Dutchman Jacob Roggeveen, stumbled upon the island of Rapa Iti in the Austral Islands during his voyage to the South Pacific. Roggeveen's encounter with the island on Easter Sunday in 1722 earned it the name "Easter Island," though it is worth noting that Easter Island is not part of French Polynesia.

The first recorded European landing on an island within present-day French Polynesia occurred in 1767. The British navigator Samuel Wallis, commanding the HMS Dolphin, made landfall on Tahiti, the largest island in the Society Islands. He named the island "King George III Island" and claimed it for Britain.

The following year, in 1768, another significant expedition reached the islands. The French explorer Louis Antoine de Bougainville, aboard the ship La Boudeuse, sighted Tahiti, where he and his crew made a brief stop before continuing their voyage. Bougainville's accounts of the islands and their inhabitants further fueled European interest in the South Pacific.

However, it was the arrival of the renowned British explorer Captain James Cook that significantly impacted the course of European involvement in the region. Cook's first voyage to the South Pacific, which began in 1768, aimed to observe the transit of Venus across the sun and to search for the fabled southern continent. During this expedition, Cook and his crew made a momentous landing on Tahiti in April 1769, allowing them to observe the transit successfully.

After leaving Tahiti, Cook's voyages took him further east, and in 1773, he became the first European to sight and map the island of Huahine in the Society Islands. Cook's detailed and accurate charts of the islands facilitated subsequent European explorations and increased their knowledge of the region.

The significance of these early European contacts extended beyond mere exploration. The interactions between European explorers and the Polynesians had a profound impact on the indigenous cultures. European trade goods, such as metal tools, firearms, and fabrics, were introduced to the islands, influencing traditional Polynesian ways of life.

The arrival of European missionaries in the 19th century further transformed the social and religious landscape of French Polynesia. Christianity began to take hold, and many Polynesians converted to the new faith, leaving behind some of their traditional beliefs and practices.

Despite these early contacts, formal European colonization of French Polynesia did not occur until the late 19th century. In 1880, the French annexed Tahiti and its neighboring islands, marking the beginning of colonial rule in the region.

Colonial Era: French Influence and Impact on the Islands

The colonial era in French Polynesia marks a pivotal period in the islands' history when French influence began to take hold, shaping the political, economic, and cultural landscape of the region. It was a time of significant change, as the islands transitioned from being independent societies to becoming part of the French colonial empire.

French interest in the islands of French Polynesia intensified in the 19th century, driven by strategic considerations, economic opportunities, and a desire for territorial expansion. In 1842, Tahiti and its neighboring islands officially became a protectorate of France, granting the French government certain rights over the islands' affairs while maintaining the indigenous monarch's authority. Throughout the colonial era, the French presence in French Polynesia gradually expanded, with military garrisons established on key islands to protect French interests and maintain control over the region. The French also sought to assert their dominance by imposing their laws, language, and customs on the native population, leading to the assimilation of many aspects of French culture.

One of the significant impacts of French colonization was the introduction of Western education and governance systems. Schools were established, and the French language was promoted as the medium of instruction, leading to a decline in the use of indigenous languages over time. The French administration also restructured the islands' political systems, replacing traditional chiefs with appointed administrators loyal to the French government.

The colonial era also saw the expansion of the plantation economy, with the French introducing cash crops such as coffee, sugarcane, and vanilla. Large tracts of land were converted into plantations, leading to changes in landownership and traditional agricultural practices. The introduction of European technologies and farming methods also influenced the islands' economic activities. In the late 19th century, French Polynesia became a destination for convict labor, with some prisoners transported from France to work on plantations or public projects in the colonies.

This influx of convict laborers had both positive and negative effects on the islands, as it provided a source of cheap labor but also led to tensions between the convicts and the local population.

The colonial period also witnessed the gradual decline of traditional Polynesian religious practices and the widespread adoption of Christianity. French missionaries played a crucial role in promoting Christianity, and many Polynesians converted to the new faith. As a result, Christian churches and places of worship became central to community life and played a significant role in shaping cultural norms.

The French colonial government also sought to exploit the islands' natural resources, particularly copra, which is the dried kernel of coconuts used for extracting coconut oil. Copra production became a major economic activity, and the islands' economy became increasingly dependent on this export.

The impact of French colonization was not uniform across all the islands, with some areas experiencing greater assimilation and acculturation than others. For instance, the Marquesas Islands, due to their remote location and rugged terrain, retained a more distinct and isolated Polynesian culture compared to the more accessible and populated Society Islands.

As the 20th century dawned, the call for more autonomy and self-governance grew among the Polynesian population. In the 1940s, the French Polynesian Assembly was established, providing the islands with a degree of local governance. However, it wasn't until the late 20th century that significant steps towards self-governance were taken, leading to the establishment of the Territorial Assembly and the appointment of French Polynesia's first president. The colonial era in French Polynesia came to an end in 1957 when the islands were reclassified as an overseas territory of France. This change in status granted French Polynesia more autonomy while remaining tied to the French Republic.

The legacy of the colonial era continues to shape the islands' identity, as French Polynesia navigates its path towards greater self-determination and cultural preservation. The interplay between French influence and Polynesian heritage has created a unique blend of cultures and traditions that define the enchanting mosaic that is French Polynesia today.

Path to Autonomy: French Polynesia's Political Evolution

As the colonial era waned, French Polynesia embarked on a journey towards greater autonomy and self-governance. This period of political evolution saw the islands gradually assert their identity and aspirations, seeking to shape their own destiny within the framework of the French Republic.

In 1946, the islands of French Polynesia were officially designated as an overseas territory of France, affording them a degree of representation in the French Parliament. This marked the beginning of a new era in the islands' political history, as they gained a voice in national decision-making.

The demand for more autonomy and a stronger local government grew throughout the mid-20th century. In response, the French Polynesian Assembly was established in 1949, providing a platform for the islands' representatives to discuss and address local issues. This move represented a significant step towards self-governance and a greater say in the islands' affairs.

The 1960s saw a rise in nationalist sentiments in French Polynesia, with calls for further political reforms and recognition of the islands' distinct identity. In 1963, the French government granted French Polynesia the status of an overseas country, providing the islands with a greater level of autonomy in certain areas, such as education and culture.

Amidst these developments, a significant political figure emerged in French Polynesia's history – Pouvanaa Oopa. Oopa was a charismatic and influential leader who advocated for greater political rights and social justice for the indigenous Polynesian population. His efforts to promote autonomy and challenge colonial policies earned him both widespread support and opposition from the French authorities.

However, in 1965, Oopa's political career took a dramatic turn when he was accused of inciting violence during protests and was subsequently arrested and imprisoned. His arrest and trial sparked controversies and allegations of political manipulation by the French government. The case remains a point of contention in

French Polynesia's political history, with debates surrounding the true motivations behind Oopa's prosecution.

In 1977, French Polynesia was granted an additional level of autonomy, transforming the islands into an overseas territory with its own government and president. The creation of the Territorial Assembly marked a significant turning point, allowing the islands to make decisions on various matters, including economic development and cultural preservation.

Throughout the 1980s and 1990s, French Polynesia experienced shifts in political leadership and governance, with different parties and leaders vying for power. The islands' political landscape became increasingly dynamic, reflecting the diversity of voices and opinions within the population.

In 2004, French Polynesia attained yet another level of autonomy with the signing of the Organic Law, further devolving powers from the French government to the local authorities. This law granted the islands greater control over issues such as immigration, land use, and natural resources.

The pursuit of self-determination and full independence has remained a topic of discussion and debate in French Polynesia. Various political parties and movements have called for referendums on independence, expressing the desire for complete sovereignty and self-governance. However, the path to independence is not without its complexities, as it involves numerous legal, economic, and political considerations.

In 2013, the French Polynesian government held a non-binding referendum on independence, in which a majority voted in favor of greater autonomy but not full independence. This outcome reflected the diverse opinions within the islands' population, with some advocating for stronger ties with France and others seeking complete sovereignty.

Modern Governance: The Structure of the Territorial Government

In the modern era, French Polynesia has evolved into a unique political entity with a distinct system of governance. The territory's government operates within the framework of the French Republic, combining elements of local autonomy with oversight from the French central government.

French Polynesia is an overseas collectivity of France, and its political structure reflects this special status. The governing system is characterized by a blend of French legal principles and traditional Polynesian customs. As an overseas collectivity, French Polynesia has its own government and institutions, enabling it to make decisions on a range of matters, including education, health, transportation, and culture.

At the helm of the territorial government is the President of French Polynesia. The President is the head of state and government, serving as the highest-ranking official in the territory. The President is elected by the members of the Territorial Assembly and holds significant powers, including the authority to appoint the government's ministers.

The Territorial Assembly is the legislative body responsible for crafting and passing laws that govern the territory. It consists of 57 members who are elected by popular vote for a five-year term. The members represent various political parties and movements, reflecting the diverse voices and opinions within French Polynesia's population.

The territorial government is organized into ministries, each headed by a minister responsible for specific areas of public policy. These ministries oversee various sectors, such as education, health, tourism, economic development, and environmental conservation. The ministers are appointed by the President and work together to implement the government's agenda.

The government's administrative structure also includes the High Commissioner of the French Republic in French Polynesia. The High Commissioner represents the French central government and ensures that French laws and policies are upheld in the territory.

The High Commissioner serves as a link between the French government and the territorial government, ensuring that decisions made in French Polynesia align with French legal frameworks.

One essential aspect of modern governance in French Polynesia is the recognition of traditional Polynesian customs and institutions. Local communities and leaders play a vital role in the decision-making process, particularly on matters concerning land use, natural resources, and cultural preservation. This recognition of traditional customs is an essential component of the territory's political identity, reflecting the desire to balance local autonomy with the values and heritage of the Polynesian people.

In recent years, there have been discussions and debates about the future political status of French Polynesia. Some political parties and movements continue to advocate for greater autonomy and independence, while others argue for maintaining the current relationship with France.

The political landscape in French Polynesia is dynamic and ever-evolving, reflecting the territory's diverse population and aspirations. As the islands move forward, they face the challenge of striking a delicate balance between preserving their unique cultural identity and navigating the benefits and responsibilities of being an overseas collectivity of France.

The structure of the Territorial Government of French Polynesia embodies the complexities and challenges of modern governance in the territory. The system seeks to uphold both French legal principles and traditional Polynesian customs, creating a distinctive blend of political and cultural influences that define the islands' identity. As the islands continue to chart their path into the future, the evolution of their political governance will undoubtedly be shaped by the changing dynamics of local and international influences, as well as the collective vision of the Polynesian people.

Flora and Fauna: Exploring the Rich Wildlife of French Polynesia

French Polynesia, with its lush tropical landscapes and pristine blue waters, is a biodiversity hotspot teeming with unique and fascinating flora and fauna. The islands' isolation in the vast expanse of the South Pacific has led to the evolution of many distinct species found nowhere else on Earth. From lush rainforests to vibrant coral reefs, French Polynesia offers a captivating array of wildlife waiting to be discovered.

The islands' forests are home to a diverse range of plant species, many of which are endemic, meaning they are found exclusively in this region. Towering coconut palms, majestic breadfruit trees, and aromatic tiare flowers are just a few examples of the plant life that adorns the landscapes of French Polynesia. The tropical rainforests are a sanctuary for an abundance of plant species, providing essential habitats for the islands' unique wildlife.

Among the most iconic residents of the French Polynesian forests is the Tiare Apetahi, a rare and delicate flower found solely on the island of Raiatea in the Society Islands. It is so revered that picking this flower is strictly prohibited, adding to its allure and significance to the local culture.

One of the most celebrated plants in French Polynesia is the Tiare Tahiti, a fragrant gardenia flower that serves as the national flower of the territory. Its delightful scent has earned it the nickname "the queen of flowers," and it is commonly used to make leis, a symbol of hospitality and affection in Polynesian culture.

The marine life in the waters surrounding French Polynesia is equally diverse and mesmerizing. The coral reefs that fringe the islands are home to a kaleidoscope of colorful fish, including parrotfish, butterflyfish, angelfish, and triggerfish. The reefs are also inhabited by graceful rays, gentle sea turtles, and the elusive and enigmatic blacktip reef sharks.

French Polynesia is famous for its encounters with majestic humpback whales during their migration season, as these gentle giants visit the warm waters to breed and give birth. Witnessing the playful acrobatics and haunting songs of these magnificent creatures is an unforgettable experience for visitors to the islands.

Beyond the coral reefs, French Polynesia boasts a wide array of marine ecosystems, including seagrass beds and mangrove forests. These habitats provide crucial nursery areas for various marine species, supporting the region's overall marine biodiversity.

The birdlife of French Polynesia is equally impressive, with many endemic species of birds taking to the skies above the islands. The Tahiti Monarch, also known as the Pomarea nigra, is a critically endangered bird found only on the island of Tahiti. Conservation efforts have been underway to protect this rare species and other endangered bird species in the region.

The islands' forests are also home to unique bird species, such as the Marquesan Kingfisher and the Fatu Hiva Monarch, both of which are endemic to the Marquesas Islands. These birds play vital roles in the ecological balance of their respective ecosystems.

One of the most peculiar and fascinating creatures found in French Polynesia is the coconut crab, also known as the robber crab. These massive land crabs can grow to an impressive size and are known for their ability to climb coconut trees to feast on the fruit, hence their name. Coconut crabs are essential for seed dispersal and play a crucial role in the health of the islands' ecosystems.

French Polynesia's diverse ecosystems are not only vital for the survival of its unique wildlife but also for the well-being of the local communities. The Polynesian people have a deep connection with nature, and many traditional practices and cultural ceremonies are centered around the islands' natural resources and wildlife.

Gastronomic Delights: Savory Cuisine of the Islands

In the culinary world, French Polynesia is a treasure trove of flavors and tastes, offering a delectable array of dishes that reflect the islands' rich cultural heritage and abundant natural resources. The cuisine of French Polynesia is a delightful fusion of traditional Polynesian ingredients and French culinary techniques, resulting in a unique and savory dining experience.

At the heart of French Polynesian cuisine is the use of fresh, locally sourced ingredients that celebrate the islands' bountiful land and sea. Coconuts, a staple in the Polynesian diet, feature prominently in many dishes, providing rich flavors and creamy textures. From coconut milk used in curries and sauces to grated coconut flesh incorporated into desserts, the versatility of this tropical fruit is a testament to its significance in the islands' culinary traditions.

Fish and seafood play a central role in the cuisine, reflecting the islands' close connection to the ocean. Mahi-mahi, tuna, grouper, and parrotfish are just a few examples of the abundant marine life that graces the tables of French Polynesians. Raw fish dishes, such as poisson cru, are especially popular, where fresh fish is marinated in lime juice and coconut milk, then mixed with vegetables and herbs for a refreshing and flavorful delight.

Another iconic dish is the Tahitian delicacy known as fafaru. This unique preparation involves fermenting fish or seafood with seawater and freshly grated coconut, resulting in a tangy and pungent flavor that is an acquired taste for some, but highly cherished by locals.

Taro, a starchy root vegetable, is a dietary staple in French Polynesia and is used in a variety of dishes. Whether boiled, mashed, or made into a traditional dish called poe, taro provides a hearty and filling component to many meals. Poe, a delightful dessert made from taro, coconut milk, and sugar, showcases the islanders' culinary creativity and love for naturally sweet and earthy flavors.

Pigs are raised and valued in traditional Polynesian culture, and their presence is reflected in the cuisine as well. The famous dish known as "himaa" is a feast cooked in an underground oven called an "imu." Whole pigs, along with other meats and vegetables, are wrapped in banana leaves and slow-cooked in the imu, resulting in tender and flavorful dishes that are enjoyed during festive occasions and gatherings.

French influences can be seen in the use of bread and pastries in Polynesian cuisine. The French introduced the art of baking to the islands, and today, baguettes and croissants are a common sight in local bakeries and breakfast tables. A popular French-inspired dish is the Poisson Cru Baguette, where poisson cru is served in a freshly baked baguette, providing a delightful fusion of French and Polynesian flavors.

When it comes to beverages, coconuts play a prominent role once again. Freshly harvested coconuts provide refreshing coconut water, while coconut milk is used to create creamy cocktails and punches. Pineapple, mango, and passion fruit are also abundant in French Polynesia, resulting in flavorful fruit juices and tropical cocktails that perfectly complement the sunny island vibes.

To complement the culinary journey, traditional Polynesian dance and music often accompany meals in the form of lively performances and cultural displays. The fusion of food, dance, and music creates a truly immersive dining experience that captures the spirit and essence of French Polynesia.

As tourism has grown in the islands, restaurants and resorts have embraced the diverse flavors of French Polynesia, creating menus that showcase the best of the local produce and culinary traditions. From beachside barbecue feasts to elegant fine dining, travelers have the opportunity to savor the many gastronomic delights that French Polynesia has to offer.

Traditional Dishes: A Culinary Journey into Local Specialties

Embarking on a culinary journey through French Polynesia means diving into a world of traditional dishes that delight the taste buds and reflect the rich cultural heritage of the islands. The traditional cuisine of French Polynesia is a tantalizing fusion of local ingredients, indigenous cooking methods, and centuries-old traditions passed down through generations.

One of the most iconic dishes in French Polynesia is poisson cru, a refreshing and vibrant dish that showcases the bounty of the islands' pristine waters. This delicacy, also known as "Tahitian ceviche," consists of raw fish, usually tuna or mahi-mahi, marinated in lime juice and mixed with freshly grated coconut and diced vegetables. The combination of zesty lime, creamy coconut, and the delicate flavor of the fish creates a harmonious and delightful taste that captures the essence of island living.

Another traditional favorite is the dish known as "mitihue," a mouthwatering blend of sweet and savory flavors. Mitihue features a combination of taro, breadfruit, or sweet potato, cooked with coconut milk and sweetened with sugar or honey. This delightful treat is often served as a dessert or side dish, offering a comforting and satisfying taste of Polynesian cuisine.

When it comes to savory dishes, "ma'a tinito" is a true Polynesian feast that brings people together for a communal dining experience. Ma'a tinito involves cooking various meats, vegetables, and seafood in an underground oven called "ahima'a." The food is wrapped in banana leaves and placed in the ahima'a, where it is slowly cooked with hot stones, infusing the ingredients with smoky and earthy flavors. Ma'a tinito is typically prepared for special occasions and celebrations, and it reflects the deep sense of community and cultural pride in Polynesian gatherings.

Seafood lovers will rejoice in the delightful flavors of "firi firi," a traditional side dish that perfectly complements seafood dishes. Firi firi are deep-fried coconut doughnuts, made with grated coconut, flour, and sugar. These delectable treats are crispy on the outside and soft on the inside, offering a sweet and savory contrast that adds a delightful touch to any meal.

For those seeking a hearty and satisfying meal, "fe'i" is a traditional dish that is sure to impress. Fe'i features roasted or boiled bananas, often served alongside fish or pork. The sweetness of the bananas and the savory flavors of the accompanying protein create a delightful and comforting combination that is deeply rooted in the Polynesian culinary heritage.

No culinary journey through French Polynesia would be complete without indulging in the delectable "po'e." Po'e is a traditional dessert made from taro or pumpkin, mixed with coconut milk, sugar, and vanilla, and then baked to perfection. The result is a luscious and fragrant pudding that captivates the senses and offers a taste of paradise with every spoonful.

To accompany the delicious dishes, traditional Polynesian beverages add a refreshing touch to the dining experience. Freshly harvested coconuts provide rejuvenating coconut water, and coconut milk is used to create creamy and delightful tropical cocktails. Pineapple, mango, and passion fruit juices offer vibrant and tangy flavors that perfectly complement the island vibes.

Exploring the traditional dishes of French Polynesia is not just a gastronomic experience; it's an opportunity to delve into the cultural richness and traditions that define the islands. Each dish tells a story of the Polynesian people's connection to the land and sea, their resourcefulness in using locally sourced ingredients, and their warm hospitality that they share with visitors.

Tahitian Cuisine: The Signature Flavors of the Islands

Tahitian cuisine is a vibrant and alluring tapestry of flavors that tantalizes the taste buds and immerses diners in the cultural richness of the islands. As the largest and most well-known archipelago in French Polynesia, Tahiti boasts a culinary heritage that is both distinct and deeply rooted in its Polynesian traditions.

At the heart of Tahitian cuisine is an appreciation for fresh and locally sourced ingredients, celebrating the bounty of the land and sea. The island's tropical climate and fertile soils provide an abundance of fruits, vegetables, and root crops that form the foundation of many Tahitian dishes.

Coconuts reign supreme in Tahitian cuisine, with various parts of the coconut tree being used in a multitude of ways. Coconut milk, extracted from grated coconut flesh, is a fundamental ingredient in many dishes, adding a rich and creamy texture. The refreshing coconut water is a popular beverage, enjoyed both on its own and as a base for tropical cocktails.

Fish and seafood are staples in Tahitian cuisine, reflecting the islands' close connection to the ocean. Freshly caught fish, such as tuna, mahi-mahi, and parrotfish, are often at the center of meals. Tahitian ceviche, known locally as "poisson cru," is a beloved dish that combines raw fish marinated in lime juice and mixed with coconut milk, cucumbers, tomatoes, and onions for a zesty and refreshing flavor.

Tahitians also take pride in their traditional dishes cooked in an ahima'a, an underground oven heated by hot stones. Ahima'a cooking infuses the food with smoky and earthy flavors, enhancing the taste of meats, vegetables, and even breadfruit. Ma'a Tahiti, a feast prepared in the ahima'a, is a special occasion dish often enjoyed during celebrations and gatherings, embodying the spirit of community and togetherness.

Taro, a starchy root vegetable, is a dietary staple in Tahiti, featured in various forms in many dishes. From being boiled and mashed to creating the traditional dessert known as "po'e," taro's versatility is evident in Tahitian cuisine. Po'e is a delightful pudding made from taro or pumpkin, blended with coconut milk, sugar, and vanilla, then baked to perfection, offering a delectable and aromatic treat.

In addition to seafood and taro, Tahitians have a fondness for pork. The island's pig farming tradition is celebrated in dishes such as "fe'i," where roasted or boiled bananas are served alongside succulent and flavorful pork. This sweet and savory combination highlights the island's ability to blend flavors in an artful and delicious way.

Tahitian cuisine also incorporates French influences, a testament to the islands' colonial history. French pastries, bread, and wines have found their way onto Tahitian tables, adding a touch of European flair to the local culinary scene. Baguettes and croissants are commonly found in local bakeries, and traditional dishes like the "Poisson Cru Baguette" fuse French and Polynesian flavors to create a unique and delightful experience.

Beyond the tantalizing flavors, Tahitian cuisine is also about the cultural experience of dining. Meals are often enjoyed communally, bringing together family and friends to share food, stories, and laughter. Traditional dance and music performances often accompany meals, adding a sensory feast to the dining experience and providing a deeper connection to the islands' vibrant culture.

Top Tourist Attractions: Must-Visit Gems of French Polynesia

French Polynesia is a tropical paradise that beckons travelers from around the world with its breathtaking landscapes, turquoise lagoons, and vibrant cultural heritage. This enchanting archipelago comprises 118 islands, each offering a unique and unforgettable experience for visitors. From pristine beaches to lush rainforests, here are some of the top tourist attractions that make French Polynesia a must-visit gem:

Bora Bora: Known as the "Pearl of the Pacific," Bora Bora is a postcard-perfect destination that captures the imagination. Its iconic overwater bungalows, surrounded by crystal-clear lagoons and a stunning volcanic peak, Mount Otemanu, create a dreamlike setting for a romantic escape or a luxurious vacation.

Moorea: Just a short ferry ride from Tahiti, Moorea is a lush and green island that boasts majestic mountains, cascading waterfalls, and serene beaches. The island offers a wealth of outdoor activities, from hiking and snorkeling to dolphin and whale watching.

Tahiti: As the largest and most populous island in French Polynesia, Tahiti serves as the gateway to the archipelago. Papeete, the capital city, is a bustling hub where visitors can explore local markets, museums, and historic sites. The island's black sand beaches and vibrant nightlife also offer a perfect blend of urban and natural experiences.

Rangiroa: Known for its immense lagoon, Rangiroa is a haven for diving enthusiasts and those seeking a tranquil escape. The Tiputa Pass, a natural channel connecting the lagoon to the open sea, provides thrilling drift dives and the chance to encounter sharks, dolphins, and rays.

Taha'a: Often referred to as the "Vanilla Island," Taha'a is renowned for its fragrant vanilla plantations and tranquil atmosphere. This secluded paradise is ideal for those seeking relaxation and immersion in the laid-back Polynesian way of life.

Huahine: With its lush landscapes and archaeological sites, Huahine offers a glimpse into the ancient Polynesian culture.

Visitors can explore ancient temples, hike through dense forests, and experience the island's unspoiled beauty.

Fakarava: This UNESCO Biosphere Reserve is a haven for nature lovers and diving enthusiasts. The pristine coral reefs teem with marine life, including sharks, dolphins, and colorful tropical fish, providing an unforgettable underwater adventure.

Marquesas Islands: Located in the northern part of French Polynesia, the Marquesas Islands offer a rugged and remote experience for intrepid travelers. Known for their dramatic landscapes and captivating cultural heritage, these islands provide a glimpse into Polynesia's ancient past.

Aitutaki: Although not officially part of French Polynesia, Aitutaki in the Cook Islands is often included in many itineraries due to its proximity and stunning beauty. Its turquoise lagoon and motus (small islets) create an idyllic setting for water-based activities and relaxation.

The Paul Gauguin Cruise: For a truly unique way to explore French Polynesia, consider a cruise aboard The Paul Gauguin, a luxury ship designed to navigate the shallow lagoons and secluded bays of the islands. This intimate cruising experience offers the opportunity to visit multiple destinations in French Polynesia while enjoying top-notch amenities and personalized service.

From romantic getaways to thrilling adventures, French Polynesia offers an array of attractions that cater to every traveler's desires. Whether snorkeling in vibrant coral gardens, exploring ancient archaeological sites, or simply basking in the serenity of a private overwater bungalow, this tropical paradise promises an unforgettable and transformative experience. With its natural beauty, warm hospitality, and captivating culture, French Polynesia stands as a beacon of allure and wonder, beckoning travelers to discover its hidden gems and create cherished memories that last a lifetime.

Bora Bora: The Ultimate Island Paradise

Nestled in the heart of the South Pacific Ocean, Bora Bora reigns as the epitome of island paradise. Its very name evokes images of crystal-clear turquoise waters, powdery white sand beaches, and overwater bungalows stretching out over the lagoon. As one of the most sought-after destinations in the world, Bora Bora lives up to its reputation as a dreamlike haven that captivates the senses and leaves an indelible mark on the hearts of all who venture to its shores.

Located in French Polynesia, Bora Bora is a tiny island in the Society Islands archipelago. It is part of the Leeward Islands group, which also includes Tahiti and Moorea. The island is surrounded by a vibrant coral reef, creating a mesmerizing lagoon known for its iridescent shades of blue and green. This stunning natural barrier ensures calm waters within the lagoon, making it an ideal playground for water-based activities and a safe haven for marine life.

The centerpiece of Bora Bora's allure is the majestic Mount Otemanu, a dormant volcano that towers over the island at 2,385 feet (727 meters) above sea level. The rugged beauty of the mountain, clothed in lush vegetation, adds a dramatic backdrop to the serene lagoon and sets the stage for breathtaking vistas that leave visitors awe-inspired.

The island's resorts and accommodations are legendary for their luxurious overwater bungalows, where guests can step directly from their bedrooms into the warm embrace of the lagoon. These iconic accommodations offer an unparalleled experience of living above the water, surrounded by the mesmerizing marine life and the soothing sounds of gentle waves lapping against the stilts.

For those who prefer to stay on land, Bora Bora offers an array of equally luxurious beachfront villas and bungalows, nestled amidst tropical gardens and fringed by swaying palm trees. From these tranquil hideaways, guests can savor the sight of stunning sunrises and sunsets over the horizon, creating a sense of serenity and connection with nature that is unmatched.

The activities in Bora Bora cater to every taste and desire. The lagoon beckons visitors to indulge in snorkeling, swimming, paddleboarding, and kayaking, revealing a vibrant underwater world teeming with colorful fish, rays, sharks, and coral gardens. Diving enthusiasts can explore the deeper waters surrounding the island, encountering the gentle giants of the sea—whale sharks and manta rays during the appropriate seasons.

Romantic excursions, such as sunset cruises and private beach dinners, offer couples the chance to bask in the enchantment of the island's natural beauty and savor moments of intimate connection amidst this idyllic setting.

For those seeking adventure, hiking trails lead to viewpoints that reveal panoramic vistas of the lagoon and the lush landscapes of the island. A visit to the Bora Bora Lagoonarium offers an opportunity to swim alongside rays and sharks in a controlled environment, providing a thrilling yet safe encounter with these majestic creatures.

The island's culture and history are also woven into its fabric, adding depth to the enchantment of Bora Bora. Visitors can explore ancient Polynesian temples, known as marae, which serve as reminders of the island's spiritual and cultural past. Traditional dance performances and local arts and crafts displays showcase the creativity and vibrant heritage of the Tahitian people.

In addition to its natural beauty and cultural richness, Bora Bora is celebrated for its culinary delights. The island's restaurants and resorts offer an array of gourmet dining experiences that celebrate the finest ingredients sourced from land and sea. From fresh seafood platters to succulent tropical fruits, the cuisine of Bora Bora tantalizes the taste buds and creates a sensory journey that complements the visual and auditory splendors of the island.

Bora Bora is not merely a destination; it is an experience that touches the soul and captures the essence of paradise. The allure of this island gem lies not only in its natural beauty but also in its ability to evoke a profound sense of tranquility and wonder. From the moment visitors arrive, they are enveloped in an aura of serenity and enchantment that permeates every aspect of the island's offerings. Bora Bora is a place where dreams become reality and memories are etched into the heart, a true testament to the ultimate island paradise that continues to beckon travelers to its shores, promising an unforgettable journey of discovery, romance, and rejuvenation.

Moorea: Enchanting Landscapes and Adventure

Nestled just a short ferry ride away from Tahiti, Moorea stands as a captivating jewel in the crown of French Polynesia. With its lush landscapes, stunning mountain peaks, and azure lagoons, Moorea is a paradise for nature lovers and adventure seekers alike. This enchanting island beckons travelers to step into a world of breathtaking beauty and exhilarating activities that create unforgettable memories and leave a lasting impression on the soul.

As part of the Society Islands archipelago, Moorea boasts a landscape that is both dramatic and serene. The island's two towering mountain peaks, known as "The Sisters" or "Les Deux Mamelles," rise majestically from the center of the island, creating a mesmerizing focal point that can be seen from various vantage points across Moorea.

The lush valleys and dense tropical forests that blanket the island add to its charm, providing an opportunity for exploration and hiking adventures. Hiking trails lead to panoramic viewpoints, such as the Belvedere Lookout, where visitors are rewarded with sweeping vistas of the island's jagged peaks, tranquil lagoons, and the distant island of Tahiti on the horizon.

Moorea's beaches are equally captivating, with powdery white sands and clear turquoise waters inviting visitors to bask in the warmth of the sun and wade into the gentle embrace of the lagoon. Snorkeling in the vibrant coral gardens reveals an underwater world teeming with colorful marine life, from playful fish to graceful rays gliding through the water.

For the adventurous at heart, Moorea offers an array of exhilarating activities that cater to all interests and skill levels. One of the most thrilling experiences on the island is swimming with sharks and rays in their natural habitat. Guided tours take visitors to the shallow waters of the lagoon, where they can safely encounter these majestic creatures up close, creating memories that will be etched into their hearts forever.

Surfing enthusiasts flock to Moorea to catch the waves at the popular Haapiti surf break, where the island's strong currents and reef breaks provide a challenge and thrill for experienced surfers. For those new to the sport, there are surf schools that offer lessons, ensuring that everyone can experience the joy of riding the waves.

Moorea's waters are also a playground for other water-based activities, including paddleboarding, kayaking, and sailing. Visitors can rent equipment or join guided tours to explore the island's stunning coastline and hidden coves, where secluded beaches and picturesque spots await discovery.

For a deeper connection with the island's marine life, scuba diving excursions reveal the wonders of the underwater world, with colorful coral reefs, abundant fish, and the occasional encounter with dolphins and sharks adding to the sense of adventure and wonder.

The island's interior offers opportunities for off-road expeditions and quad biking, taking visitors on thrilling journeys through rugged terrain, lush vegetation, and untamed landscapes. These excursions provide a unique perspective of Moorea's natural beauty and a chance to immerse in its wild heart.

In addition to its natural attractions, Moorea is also a haven for cultural experiences. Visitors can explore local markets, artisan workshops, and traditional dance performances that showcase the island's vibrant heritage and the warm hospitality of its people.

Moorea's culinary offerings are equally delightful, with restaurants and resorts serving an array of dishes that celebrate local ingredients and traditional Polynesian flavors. Fresh seafood, tropical fruits, and flavorsome dishes create a delectable dining experience that complements the island's allure.

Tahiti: Heartbeat of French Polynesia

At the heart of French Polynesia lies the beating pulse of the South Pacific—the mesmerizing island of Tahiti. Revered as the largest and most populous island in the archipelago, Tahiti is a vibrant tapestry of culture, natural beauty, and warm hospitality. With its lush landscapes, captivating traditions, and bustling capital city, Papeete, Tahiti stands as the gateway to a world of exploration and enchantment.

Tahiti's allure begins with its diverse landscapes, ranging from emerald green valleys and cascading waterfalls to black sand beaches and turquoise lagoons. The island is a volcanic wonder, shaped by ancient eruptions that forged its jagged peaks and fertile valleys. Mount Orohena, the highest point in French Polynesia, stands proudly at 7,352 feet (2,241 meters), offering a majestic backdrop to the island's natural beauty.

Papeete, the bustling capital city, is the heartbeat of Tahiti. The city's vibrant markets, including Le Marché de Papeete, offer a feast for the senses, with colorful displays of tropical fruits, handcrafted pareos, and fragrant flowers. Visitors can immerse themselves in the local culture, interacting with friendly vendors and savoring the flavors of Tahitian cuisine, such as "poisson cru," a refreshing dish of raw fish marinated in lime juice and coconut milk.

Tahiti's cultural heritage is deeply ingrained in the everyday lives of its people. Traditional dance and music, including the iconic "tamure" dance, are an integral part of Tahitian celebrations and festivals. Through the mesmerizing movements of dance and the rhythm of drums, the island's history and myths come alive, honoring the spirit of the ancient Polynesian ancestors.

The island's marae, or sacred temples, are sacred sites that hold historical and spiritual significance for the Tahitian people. These stone structures are vestiges of a rich cultural legacy, serving as a link to the past and a testament to the island's profound spiritual connections with the land and sea.

Tahiti's shores are adorned with black sand beaches, a unique feature that sets the island apart from other tropical destinations. The volcanic nature of the island gives rise to these striking beaches, creating a dramatic contrast against the azure waters of the lagoon.

The island's lagoon is a haven for water-based activities, from snorkeling and diving to paddleboarding and sailing. The coral reefs teem with colorful marine life, including tropical fish, rays, and sharks, providing a captivating underwater world for exploration.

As the sun sets over Tahiti, a sense of serenity envelops the island. The twilight hues paint the sky with an ethereal glow, casting a spell of tranquility that invites visitors to embrace the beauty of the moment. Tahiti's sunsets are renowned for their splendor, offering a moment of reflection and gratitude for the wonders of nature.

Tahiti's people are warm and welcoming, embodying the spirit of "Mana," a Polynesian term that refers to the spiritual energy and life force that permeates the island. This unique blend of friendliness and reverence for nature creates an atmosphere of harmony and unity, making visitors feel at home in the embrace of Tahiti's hospitality.

Beyond its natural beauty and cultural richness, Tahiti is a place where time slows down and life is savored at a leisurely pace. It is a destination for dreamers and adventurers, where exploration is met with wonder, and relaxation is a way of life.

Raiatea and Taha'a: Historical and Sacred Wonders

As we continue our journey through French Polynesia, we find ourselves drawn to the enchanting islands of Raiatea and Taha'a. Located in the Society Islands archipelago, these sister islands stand as a testament to the rich history and spiritual significance of the region. Stepping foot on these shores, visitors are transported back in time, where ancient temples, lush landscapes, and traditions steeped in mystique await exploration.

Raiatea, often referred to as the "Sacred Island," holds a special place in Polynesian mythology. It is believed to be the center of the ancient Polynesian world, where the great voyaging canoes of the past set sail to explore distant lands. The island is rich in archaeological sites, including the famous marae Taputapuātea, a UNESCO World Heritage Site and the largest religious complex in French Polynesia.

Marae Taputapuātea serves as a place of immense spiritual and cultural significance for the Tahitian people. It was once the site of important ceremonies and gatherings, where chiefs and priests would convene to make important decisions and seek the favor of the gods. Today, visitors can wander amidst the ancient stone structures, feeling the weight of history and marveling at the engineering feats of the ancient Polynesians who built these sacred sites.

Beyond its historical wonders, Raiatea is also renowned for its lush and fertile landscapes. The island is a haven for nature enthusiasts, offering hiking trails that lead to stunning viewpoints and hidden waterfalls. The Faaroa River, the only navigable river in French Polynesia, winds its way through the heart of the island, providing an opportunity for serene boat trips through dense tropical vegetation.

A short boat ride from Raiatea brings us to the tranquil island of Taha'a, often referred to as the "Vanilla Island." Taha'a is known for its bountiful vanilla plantations, where the intoxicating aroma of vanilla beans perfumes the air. Visitors can explore these fragrant plantations, learning about the intricate process of vanilla cultivation and its importance to the local economy.

Taha'a's natural beauty extends beyond its vanilla plantations, offering picturesque views of the lagoon and neighboring islands. The island's motus (small islets) are perfect for secluded picnics and snorkeling excursions, where vibrant coral gardens and marine life await beneath the surface.

In addition to its agricultural prowess, Taha'a is also home to a variety of traditional crafts. Local artisans create intricate pareos, woven hats, and other handicrafts that showcase the island's creative spirit and artistic heritage.

Like its sister island Raiatea, Taha'a is steeped in cultural traditions, with ancient marae dotting its landscapes. These sacred sites bear witness to the island's past, connecting its people with their ancestors and the stories of old.

As we explore Raiatea and Taha'a, we are reminded of the deep spiritual and historical roots that underpin the islands' allure. Here, the past and present intertwine, and the spirit of the ancient Polynesians lives on in the hearts of the people and the landscapes they inhabit.

Raiatea and Taha'a offer a captivating glimpse into the soul of French Polynesia, where sacred wonders and historical treasures coexist with the vibrant colors of nature. These sister islands beckon travelers to step off the beaten path and immerse themselves in the rich tapestry of Polynesian heritage and natural beauty. With each step, visitors draw closer to the heart of the South Pacific, where the echoes of the past resonate in the present, creating an unforgettable journey of discovery and wonder.

Huahine: The Garden of Eden

Nestled within the Society Islands of French Polynesia lies a hidden gem known as Huahine—the Garden of Eden. This enchanting island exudes a sense of untouched beauty and an aura of serenity that captivates all who set foot on its shores. With its lush landscapes, crystal-clear lagoons, and vibrant culture, Huahine offers a glimpse into a world of natural wonder and timeless traditions.

Huahine is actually composed of two islands, Huahine Nui (Big Huahine) and Huahine Iti (Little Huahine), connected by a bridge. Despite its proximity to the more well-known Tahiti and Bora Bora, Huahine has managed to retain its off-the-beaten-path allure, making it a haven for travelers seeking a more secluded and authentic experience.

Known as the "Island of Women" in ancient Polynesian legends, Huahine is steeped in mythology and history. According to the tales, the island's lush valleys and fertile soils were created by the goddess Hiro, who molded the land with her hands, bestowing it with fertility and abundant crops.

Huahine's landscapes are a harmonious blend of dense forests, verdant hills, and pristine beaches. The island is a nature lover's paradise, offering hiking trails that lead to panoramic viewpoints, where visitors are treated to sweeping vistas of turquoise lagoons and neighboring islands.

The island's lagoon is a sanctuary for marine life, boasting vibrant coral reefs that teem with an array of tropical fish, rays, and sharks. Snorkeling and diving excursions provide an opportunity to immerse in this underwater wonderland, creating a sense of awe and reverence for the wonders of the sea.

Huahine's traditional culture is deeply rooted in the daily lives of its people. The island's inhabitants take pride in preserving their heritage and customs, with traditional dance, music, and crafts playing a central role in their celebrations and rituals.

One of the most iconic symbols of Huahine is the "marae," ancient stone platforms that served as religious and ceremonial sites for the ancient Polynesians. These sacred structures are scattered throughout the island, standing as silent witnesses to a bygone era.

Huahine's laid-back and unhurried pace of life is reflected in the warmth and hospitality of its people. Visitors are welcomed with open arms, invited to partake in local traditions and festivities, and encouraged to embrace the island's spirit of "mana," a Polynesian term for spiritual energy and life force.

The island's vanilla plantations are another highlight, with Huahine being one of the major producers of this fragrant spice in French Polynesia. Visitors can tour these plantations, learning about the intricate process of vanilla cultivation and savoring the aroma of fresh vanilla beans.

Huahine's beaches are postcard-perfect, with powdery white sands meeting the gentle waves of the lagoon. Here, visitors can find their own secluded spot to unwind and immerse in the tranquility of the surroundings.

The island's main village, Fare, offers a glimpse into local life and a chance to explore the island's market, where fresh produce, handicrafts, and souvenirs can be found.

Huahine's charm lies not only in its natural beauty but also in its ability to transport visitors to a simpler and more authentic way of life. Here, time seems to stand still, allowing travelers to reconnect with nature, themselves, and the essence of the South Pacific.

Nuku Hiva and Hiva Oa: Marquesas Archipelago's Treasures

As we venture into the remote and rugged Marquesas Archipelago of French Polynesia, we discover two hidden treasures: Nuku Hiva and Hiva Oa. These islands are a world away from the more well-known tourist destinations, offering a raw and untamed beauty that captivates the soul. Here, amidst soaring cliffs, deep valleys, and ancient cultural sites, we find a true sense of adventure and discovery.

Nuku Hiva, the largest of the Marquesas islands, is a landscape of dramatic contrasts. Its mountain peaks rise majestically to touch the sky, while its lush valleys cradle serene villages and fertile lands. The island's rugged coastline is lashed by the powerful waves of the Pacific Ocean, creating striking sea cliffs and secluded coves.

At the heart of Nuku Hiva lies Taipivai Valley, made famous by the American writer Herman Melville in his novel "Typee." This lush valley is steeped in history and folklore, with ancient marae and stone structures scattered throughout the landscape, testament to the island's rich cultural heritage.

The island's capital, Taiohae, offers a glimpse into local life, where the rhythms of the community are felt in the bustling markets and vibrant festivals. Here, visitors can immerse themselves in the traditional arts and crafts of the Marquesas people, witnessing the intricate carvings and tattooing that are integral to their culture.

The surrounding waters of Nuku Hiva are teeming with marine life, making it a paradise for diving and snorkeling enthusiasts. The underwater world here is a kaleidoscope of colors, with coral reefs, schools of tropical fish, and the occasional appearance of dolphins and sharks.

A short journey southward brings us to Hiva Oa, another gem in the Marquesas Archipelago. This island is renowned for its towering volcanic peaks, including Mount Temetiu, which offers panoramic views of the island's rugged landscape and the deep blue sea beyond.

Hiva Oa is perhaps most famous for being the final resting place of two iconic artists: Paul Gauguin and Jacques Brel. Both artists were drawn to the island's remote beauty and sought refuge here, leaving behind a legacy that is still felt by visitors today. Their resting places, Calvary Cemetery for Gauguin and Atuona Cemetery for Brel, are pilgrimage sites for those seeking to pay homage to these creative geniuses.

Hiva Oa's cultural heritage is celebrated through traditional dance and music, which play an essential role in community gatherings and ceremonies. The island's festivals, such as the "mata hoata," showcase the vibrant spirit of the Marquesas people and their deep connection to the land and sea.

The island's interior is a haven for hikers and adventurers, with trails leading to hidden waterfalls, ancient petroglyphs, and sacred sites. The "Puamau Tiki," a massive stone statue standing at almost ten feet tall, is an impressive testament to the island's ancient past and a reminder of the skilled craftsmanship of its people.

While Nuku Hiva and Hiva Oa may be lesser-known destinations in French Polynesia, they offer a unique and authentic experience that is unrivaled. Here, visitors can step back in time, exploring landscapes that remain largely untouched by modernity and encountering cultures that have preserved their traditions for generations.

Rangiroa and Fakarava: Exploring the Tuamotus Atolls

As we continue our odyssey through the stunning landscapes of French Polynesia, we find ourselves drawn to the remote and captivating Tuamotus Archipelago. Here, amidst the vast expanse of the South Pacific, lie two hidden gems: Rangiroa and Fakarava. These atolls offer a unique and off-the-beaten-path experience, where turquoise lagoons, vibrant coral reefs, and a sense of tranquility abound.

Rangiroa, the largest atoll in the Tuamotus, is a natural wonder to behold. Its lagoon is one of the most expansive in the world, offering a playground for water-based activities such as snorkeling, diving, and fishing. The Tiputa and Avatoru passes, where the lagoon meets the open ocean, are famous for their strong currents and the thrilling drift dives they offer.

The underwater world of Rangiroa is teeming with marine life, from colorful tropical fish to majestic manta rays and even the occasional appearance of sharks. The Tiputa Pass is known for its encounters with bottlenose dolphins, creating unforgettable moments for divers and snorkelers alike.

Beyond its underwater wonders, Rangiroa's beaches are a picture of tranquility, with powdery white sands and crystal-clear waters inviting visitors to unwind and savor the feeling of being cast adrift in a paradise.

The island's main village, Avatoru, is a glimpse into the local way of life, where the rhythms of the community revolve around the sea and the land. Visitors can explore the village's markets, sample local delicacies, and witness the warm hospitality of the island's people.

A short flight from Rangiroa brings us to Fakarava, another jewel in the Tuamotus Atolls. Fakarava is a UNESCO Biosphere Reserve, known for its rich biodiversity and pristine natural environment. The island's main attraction is the Garuae Pass, the largest pass in French Polynesia, where divers can witness a magnificent array of marine life, including schools of sharks, rays, and colorful fish.

Fakarava's pink sand beaches add to its allure, providing a stunning contrast against the turquoise waters of the lagoon. These secluded shores offer a sense of seclusion and romance, making them perfect for quiet moments of reflection and connection with nature.

The island's villages, Rotoava and Tetamanu, offer a glimpse into the local culture and traditional way of life. Visitors can learn about the island's history and customs, as well as witness demonstrations of traditional dance and music.

Fakarava's pristine environment is a haven for eco-tourism, with opportunities for birdwatching, exploring mangrove forests, and discovering the diverse flora and fauna that call this atoll home.

Both Rangiroa and Fakarava embody the essence of the Tuamotus Atolls—remote, untouched, and abundant with natural beauty. Here, travelers can escape the bustle of modern life and immerse themselves in the tranquil rhythms of the sea and the land. The Tuamotus offer a chance to reconnect with the elemental forces of nature and find solace in the vastness of the ocean.

Humpback Whales and Dolphins: Marveling at Marine Life

As we voyage further into the pristine waters of French Polynesia, we encounter some of the most magnificent creatures of the ocean—the humpback whales and dolphins. These gentle giants and playful dolphins are a testament to the rich biodiversity that thrives in these azure waters, captivating the hearts of all who are fortunate enough to witness their majestic presence.

The warm, nutrient-rich waters of French Polynesia serve as a vital sanctuary for humpback whales during their annual migration. Each year, between July and November, these majestic mammals embark on a journey spanning thousands of miles from the cold Antarctic waters to the warm tropical seas of French Polynesia. The purpose of this arduous migration is to breed and give birth to their calves in the safe and sheltered lagoons.

One of the most remarkable phenomena of humpback whales is their haunting and melodic songs. The males are known for their elaborate and enchanting vocalizations, which can travel for great distances underwater. These complex songs are thought to play a role in mating rituals and communication within their pods.

The islands of Moorea, Tahiti, and Rurutu are among the best places to witness the majestic presence of humpback whales during their annual migration. Excursions led by experienced guides offer a once-in-a-lifetime opportunity to observe these gentle giants up close, from the safety and respect of a distance regulated by protective laws.

Witnessing a humpback whale breach, launching its massive body out of the water and crashing back with an awe-inspiring splash, is an unforgettable experience. These displays of strength and grace leave spectators in sheer amazement, reminding us of the incredible wonders that lie beneath the ocean's surface.

Dolphins are also a common sight in the waters of French Polynesia, enchanting visitors with their playful nature and acrobatic displays. Spinner dolphins, bottlenose dolphins, and rough-toothed dolphins are among the species commonly encountered in these waters.

Spinner dolphins, as their name suggests, are known for their impressive spinning leaps and aerial acrobatics. These sociable creatures often travel in large pods, leaping and somersaulting in synchrony, creating a mesmerizing spectacle that leaves observers in awe.

Bottlenose dolphins are also a popular sight, known for their friendly and curious behavior towards humans. They can be spotted swimming alongside boats, seemingly eager to interact with passengers.

Rough-toothed dolphins, with their distinctive ridged teeth, are more elusive but still occasionally encountered during marine excursions. Their sleek bodies and graceful movements make them a delight to observe.

One of the best ways to witness these intelligent marine mammals is through guided dolphin-watching tours, which follow ethical guidelines to ensure minimal disturbance to the animals' natural behaviors.

French Polynesia is committed to the conservation and protection of its marine life. Several organizations, such as the Pacific Whale Foundation, conduct research and educational initiatives to raise awareness about the importance of preserving the marine ecosystem and its inhabitants.

The opportunity to marvel at humpback whales and dolphins in their natural habitat is a humbling and awe-inspiring experience. It serves as a reminder of the delicate balance of life in the ocean and the responsibility we hold to protect and preserve these magnificent creatures for generations to come.

In the presence of humpback whales and dolphins, we are reminded of the beauty and diversity that lie beneath the waves, inviting us to appreciate the interconnectedness of all living beings and the splendor of the natural world. As we journey through the waters of French Polynesia, these encounters with marine life become cherished memories, etching the spirit of the ocean into our hearts and leaving us with a profound sense of wonder and gratitude for the wonders of marine life.

Coral Reefs: Diving into Colorful Underwater Worlds

As we descend beneath the surface of the azure waters of French Polynesia, a whole new realm of vibrant colors and breathtaking beauty awaits us—the mesmerizing world of coral reefs. These underwater ecosystems are teeming with life, offering a kaleidoscope of colors and an unparalleled diversity of marine species.

Coral reefs are among the most biologically diverse and productive ecosystems on Earth. Despite covering less than 1% of the ocean floor, they are home to an estimated 25% of all marine species, making them a true wonder of the underwater world.

The coral polyps, tiny organisms resembling delicate sea anemones, are the building blocks of these magnificent reefs. They secrete calcium carbonate to form exoskeletons, creating intricate structures that provide shelter and support for countless marine creatures.

French Polynesia's coral reefs are particularly renowned for their health and diversity. The warm tropical waters and strong ocean currents provide ideal conditions for coral growth, resulting in thriving reefs that boast an array of shapes, sizes, and colors.

Soft corals, such as the magnificent sea fans and whip corals, sway gently in the currents, adding an ethereal beauty to the underwater landscape. Hard corals, like the brain corals and table corals, form massive colonies that resemble intricate sculptures, creating a sight that is nothing short of mesmerizing.

The vibrant colors of the coral reefs are a testament to the symbiotic relationship between the coral polyps and the tiny algae known as zooxanthellae. These algae live within the tissues of the coral, providing them with essential nutrients through photosynthesis. In return, the coral offers the algae a protected environment to thrive. This mutualistic relationship is the key to the reefs' stunning hues and their ability to support such a diverse array of marine life.

French Polynesia's coral reefs are a sanctuary for a myriad of marine creatures. Schools of colorful fish, from parrotfish and butterflyfish to angelfish and surgeonfish, dart in and out of the coral formations, creating a kaleidoscope of movement and color.

Reef sharks, such as the graceful blacktip and whitetip reef sharks, can often be spotted patrolling the outer edges of the reefs, adding an element of excitement and wonder to any diving or snorkeling experience.

The coral reefs are also a crucial nursery ground for various marine species, including sea turtles and rays. Many of these animals return to the reefs throughout their lives to feed and seek shelter, highlighting the importance of preserving these delicate ecosystems.

French Polynesia is committed to protecting its coral reefs and the marine life they support. Several marine reserves and protected areas have been established to conserve the reefs and ensure sustainable practices in diving and snorkeling activities.

As visitors, it is essential to approach these underwater worlds with respect and responsibility. Following ethical diving and snorkeling guidelines, such as not touching or disturbing the coral or marine life, helps to minimize the impact on these delicate ecosystems and allows future generations to continue marveling at their beauty.

In the presence of coral reefs, we are invited into a world of wonder and discovery—a world that ignites our curiosity and leaves us humbled by the intricate dance of life beneath the waves. As we explore the colorful underwater realms of French Polynesia, we are reminded of the delicate balance of nature and our shared responsibility to protect and cherish these vibrant ecosystems for generations to come.

Traditional Arts and Crafts: Experiencing Polynesian Creativity

As we immerse ourselves in the vibrant culture of French Polynesia, we are enchanted by the richness of its traditional arts and crafts. The creativity and craftsmanship of the Polynesian people are expressed through a myriad of intricate and beautiful works, each holding a story of cultural heritage and artistic excellence.

Tahitian culture places great value on the arts, and creativity is woven into the fabric of everyday life. From the mesmerizing dance performances to the skilled craftsmanship of handmade goods, traditional arts are a living expression of the Polynesian identity.

One of the most iconic and recognizable forms of art in French Polynesia is the Tahitian dance, known as the "Ori Tahiti." This dynamic and rhythmic dance is a celebration of life, nature, and the spirit of the islands. Dancers move gracefully, expressing stories and emotions through their movements, adorned in colorful costumes and fragrant flower leis.

The crafting of these intricate costumes is itself an art form. Costumes are adorned with natural materials, such as feathers, shells, and fibers, showcasing the connection between the Polynesian people and the bountiful resources of their environment.

Tattooing is another deeply rooted form of artistic expression in French Polynesia. Traditional Polynesian tattoos, known as "tatau" or "tatu," hold immense cultural significance, representing rites of passage, social status, and personal identity. The intricate designs are hand-tapped into the skin, a testament to the skill and artistry of the tattoo artists.

Wood carving is a traditional craft that has been passed down through generations in French Polynesia. The skilled carvers create intricate sculptures, masks, and ceremonial objects, often featuring motifs inspired by nature and mythology.

The production of tapa cloth, known as "tapa" or "'ahu," is a traditional art form that dates back centuries. Made from the inner bark of the paper mulberry tree, tapa cloth is pounded, painted, and adorned with intricate designs, creating stunning and unique textiles that are used in ceremonies and as decorative items.

Another important art form is weaving, with skilled artisans creating intricate baskets, hats, and mats from pandanus and coconut fibers. These practical and beautiful items are an essential part of Polynesian life, used in daily activities and special occasions alike.

The creation of shell jewelry is yet another example of Polynesian creativity. Necklaces, bracelets, and earrings adorned with iridescent shells are popular souvenirs for visitors, carrying with them the spirit of the islands and the ocean.

French Polynesia's traditional arts and crafts are not just beautiful to behold; they also play a vital role in preserving the cultural heritage of the islands. The passing down of these artistic skills from one generation to the next ensures the continuation of age-old traditions and the celebration of the Polynesian way of life.

Visitors to French Polynesia have the unique opportunity to witness these traditional arts in action. Cultural centers, museums, and artisan markets showcase the talent and creativity of local craftsmen and dancers, providing a deeper understanding of the cultural significance behind each piece.

By participating in workshops and attending performances, travelers can become part of the living legacy of Polynesian arts and crafts, forging connections with the people and their heritage.

In the beauty of these traditional arts, we find not just works of creativity but also a glimpse into the soul of French Polynesia. The passion, skill, and reverence that go into each piece reflect the deep connection that the Polynesian people have with their land, their ancestors, and the spirit of the islands.

Music and Dance: The Rhythms of Polynesian Culture

In the heart of French Polynesia, music and dance are woven into the very essence of everyday life. The vibrant and soul-stirring rhythms of Polynesian culture resonate throughout the islands, creating a symphony of sound and movement that embodies the spirit and traditions of the people.

Music holds a special place in the hearts of the Polynesian people, serving as a way to pass down stories, celebrate life's milestones, and express deep emotions. Traditional Polynesian music is characterized by its use of percussion instruments, string instruments, and hauntingly beautiful vocals that carry the essence of the islands.

One of the most iconic musical instruments in Polynesian culture is the "pahu," a large ceremonial drum made from a hollowed-out tree trunk covered with sharkskin. The deep, resonant beats of the pahu are often accompanied by the rhythms of the "to'ere," a hollowed-out log drum, and the sweet melodies of the ukulele or guitar.

Chants, known as "himene," are an essential part of Polynesian music, carrying the oral history and cultural wisdom of the islands. These chants are performed in unison, with powerful harmonies that evoke a deep sense of unity and connection among the singers and their audience.

The "ote'a" dance is an integral part of traditional Polynesian music, characterized by the powerful and energetic movements of the dancers. Accompanied by the pulsating rhythms of drums and chants, the ote'a dance tells stories of ancient battles, legends, and the beauty of nature. Dancers sway, stomp, and leap with graceful athleticism, creating a mesmerizing spectacle that leaves spectators in awe.

In contrast to the high-energy ote'a dance, the "aparima" dance is a more subdued and graceful form of expression. Aparima is often accompanied by melodic ballads, with dancers using graceful hand movements to convey emotions and tell stories through their gestures.

French Polynesia's music and dance traditions are not static; they are living expressions that continue to evolve and adapt with the times. Today, contemporary Polynesian music incorporates elements of reggae, pop, and hip-hop, while still maintaining the essence of its cultural roots.

One of the most celebrated Polynesian musicians is Bobby Holcomb, whose songs are a fusion of traditional melodies and poetic lyrics that capture the beauty and essence of the islands. His music has transcended borders, bringing the soulful melodies of Polynesia to a global audience.

Throughout the year, festivals and cultural events showcase the richness of Polynesian music and dance. The Heiva festival, held annually in Tahiti, is a vibrant celebration of traditional arts and culture. Dancers, musicians, and artisans from across the islands come together to compete and share their talents, creating an atmosphere of camaraderie and celebration.

Tourists visiting French Polynesia have the opportunity to witness these captivating performances at resorts, cultural centers, and local events. Experiencing the music and dance of Polynesia is not just a form of entertainment but a way to connect with the heart and soul of the islands and gain a deeper understanding of their cultural heritage.

Taputapuā tea: UNESCO World Heritage Site of Marae Complex

In the heart of the Society Islands in French Polynesia lies a sacred place of immense historical and cultural significance—the Taputapuātea marae complex. Designated as a UNESCO World Heritage Site in 2017, Taputapuātea holds a revered place in the hearts of the Polynesian people, serving as a symbol of their ancestral heritage and a testament to their profound connection with the land and the cosmos.

Located on the island of Ra'iatea, Taputapuātea is one of the most important archaeological sites in the South Pacific. The marae complex spans over 11 acres and consists of several marae, or traditional Polynesian temples, along with sacred stone structures and ceremonial platforms.

The marae were central to the spiritual and social life of the ancient Polynesians. These sacred places were used for religious ceremonies, rituals, and gatherings, and served as a connection between the mortal realm and the realm of the gods.

Taputapuātea was a significant center of religious and cultural activity in ancient Polynesia, acting as the spiritual and political heart of the region. It was a place of pilgrimage for people from various islands who traveled to Ra'iatea to pay homage to their gods, seek blessings, and participate in important ceremonies.

The marae complex at Taputapuātea was dedicated to the worship of the powerful and revered god, Oro, who was associated with war, fertility, and the cycle of life. As the god of war, Oro was believed to bring victory to warriors in battle, while as the god of fertility, he played a vital role in ensuring the prosperity and abundance of the land.

The architecture of Taputapuātea reflects the intricate and precise craftsmanship of the ancient Polynesians. The stone structures were carefully constructed using massive blocks of coral and basalt, highlighting the engineering prowess of the Polynesian people. The layout of the marae complex was meticulously designed, with each area serving a specific purpose in the religious and social life of the community.

The marae at Taputapuātea were not just places of worship but also centers of learning and cultural exchange. They were venues for passing down oral history, legends, and knowledge from one generation to the next. Through ceremonies and storytelling, the ancient Polynesians preserved their cultural heritage and ensured its continuation into the future.

Taputapuātea's designation as a UNESCO World Heritage Site is a recognition of its outstanding universal value and its significance as a living testament to the enduring cultural traditions of the Polynesian people. The site serves as a reminder of the deep-rooted connection between the people, the land, and the cosmos—an essential part of their identity and way of life.

Today, Taputapuātea continues to hold a sacred place in the hearts of the Polynesian people. It is a site of cultural revival and preservation, where traditional ceremonies and rituals are still practiced, ensuring that the cultural heritage of the islands remains vibrant and alive.

Visitors to Taputapuātea have the unique opportunity to step back in time and immerse themselves in the spiritual and historical significance of the marae complex. Guided tours provide insight into the rich cultural traditions of the Polynesian people and the importance of Taputapuātea in their lives.

Heiva Festival: Celebrating Polynesian Culture

If there's one event that encapsulates the vibrant spirit and rich cultural heritage of French Polynesia, it's the Heiva Festival. This annual celebration is the pinnacle of Polynesian culture, a time when the islands come alive with traditional music, dance, sports, and art, uniting the people in a shared sense of pride and belonging.

The Heiva Festival has its roots in ancient Polynesian traditions, where communities would gather to celebrate and honor their gods through song, dance, and competitions. Over the centuries, these gatherings evolved into a more organized and elaborate event, eventually becoming the Heiva we know today.

The festival takes place during the month of July, with its main hub in Papeete, the capital of Tahiti. However, it is also celebrated in other islands across French Polynesia, each adding its unique flair and cultural elements to the festivities.

Preparations for the Heiva Festival begin months in advance, with dance groups, musicians, and sports teams diligently rehearsing their performances and perfecting their skills. Each group aims to showcase the best of their island's culture and traditions, and the competition can be fierce.

One of the highlights of the Heiva Festival is the traditional Polynesian dance competition. Dancers adorned in vibrant costumes and flower leis take the stage, performing the ote'a, aparima, and hivinau dances with grace and passion. The dances often depict historical events, myths, and legends, serving as a visual narrative of the islands' heritage.

Music plays a central role in the Heiva Festival, with live performances featuring traditional instruments like the to'ere, pahu, and ukulele. The captivating melodies and harmonies, along with the energetic drumming, transport the audience to the heart of Polynesian culture.

Sports competitions are also an integral part of the Heiva Festival, reflecting the Polynesian spirit of strength, agility, and camaraderie. Events such as outrigger canoe races, stone lifting, and traditional wrestling showcase the athletic prowess of the participants and their deep connection to the land and sea.

The Heiva Festival is not just about performances and competitions; it is a time for the Polynesian people to come together as a community, celebrating their shared heritage and strengthening their bonds. Families and friends gather to enjoy the festivities, sharing meals and laughter, creating memories that will last a lifetime.

For tourists visiting French Polynesia during the Heiva Festival, it is an unparalleled opportunity to immerse themselves in the authentic culture of the islands. Cultural performances, artisan markets, and traditional cuisine tantalize the senses and offer a glimpse into the soul of Polynesian life.

The Heiva Festival is a celebration of resilience and cultural revival. It faced periods of decline during the colonial era, but in the 20th century, efforts were made to revitalize and preserve Polynesian traditions, leading to the establishment of the modern Heiva Festival.

Today, the festival continues to evolve, embracing contemporary elements while honoring the ancient customs. It serves as a platform for passing down traditional knowledge to younger generations, ensuring the continuity of Polynesian culture for years to come.

Tiki Culture: Unraveling Ancient Symbols and Meanings

When we think of the word "Tiki," images of wooden statues, tropical cocktails, and exotic decor often come to mind. But Tiki culture is more than just a trendy theme; it is deeply rooted in the ancient beliefs and traditions of the Polynesian people.

The origins of Tiki culture can be traced back to the ancient Polynesians, who inhabited the islands of the South Pacific thousands of years ago. Tiki, in its essence, refers to the first human being in Maori and Hawaiian mythology. According to these myths, Tiki was the progenitor of humankind, and his likeness is often depicted in the form of carved wooden statues.

Tiki statues hold significant cultural and spiritual meanings for the Polynesian people. These wooden carvings represent deities, ancestors, or protective spirits, and they serve as a connection between the mortal realm and the divine. Tiki statues are often placed in sacred places, such as marae complexes, to invoke the blessings and protection of the gods.

The art of Tiki carving is a skill that has been passed down through generations in Polynesian culture. Carvers use traditional tools and techniques to transform raw wood into intricate and expressive statues. Each Tiki statue is unique, bearing the personality and energy of the carver, and the symbolism of the specific deity or ancestor it represents.

Tiki culture experienced a resurgence in popularity in the mid-20th century, particularly in the United States. The post-World War II era saw an increased fascination with all things exotic and tropical, and Tiki bars and restaurants became a popular trend, offering an escape to a mythical and mysterious paradise.

These Tiki bars often featured Polynesian-inspired decor, including bamboo furniture, thatch roofs, and, of course, Tiki statues. The ambiance was meant to transport patrons to an idyllic tropical paradise, complete with rum-based cocktails served in carved Tiki mugs.

While the Tiki culture of the mid-century was undoubtedly influenced by romanticized notions of Polynesia, it also introduced elements of Polynesian art and design to a global audience. Tiki bars became spaces where people could experience a taste of the islands' culture, even if it was a stylized version.

Today, Tiki culture continues to thrive, with a growing appreciation for its historical and cultural significance. Artists and carvers are preserving and reimagining the tradition of Tiki carving, infusing it with contemporary creativity while honoring its roots.

For the Polynesian people, Tiki culture remains a vital part of their identity and heritage. Tiki statues continue to be carved for ceremonial and religious purposes, and their presence in homes, community spaces, and cultural events serves as a reminder of the ancient connections to the gods and ancestors.

As we delve into the world of Tiki culture, we discover more than just an aesthetic or a trend. We find a rich tapestry of history, spirituality, and artistry that spans centuries. In the Tiki statues, we witness the reverence and respect that the Polynesian people hold for their cultural symbols and traditions.

Tiki culture is a bridge that connects the past with the present, offering us a glimpse into the beliefs and values of the ancient Polynesians. It invites us to appreciate the beauty of their art and the wisdom of their spirituality.

In the Tiki bars and statues that adorn modern spaces, we find more than just an escape to a tropical paradise; we find a reflection of our fascination with the exotic and the mysterious. But beneath the surface, we discover a deeper appreciation for the diverse and captivating cultures that make up our world.

Navigation and Wayfinding: Ancient Polynesian Skills

Imagine navigating vast stretches of the Pacific Ocean, thousands of miles from any visible land, with nothing but the stars, the sun, and the sea as your guide. For the ancient Polynesians, this was not just a feat of bravery; it was a testament to their remarkable navigational skills and deep understanding of the natural world.

Long before the invention of modern navigation tools like GPS and compasses, the Polynesians relied on their innate knowledge of the stars, winds, currents, and natural landmarks to traverse the vast expanse of the Pacific Ocean. Their wayfinding techniques were not just a practical means of transportation but a cultural tradition, passed down through generations and revered as an essential part of their identity.

Central to Polynesian navigation was their intimate knowledge of the stars. By observing the night sky, they could determine their latitude and direction. They learned to identify key constellations and used them as celestial landmarks to guide their journeys. The rising and setting positions of certain stars helped them gauge their east-west direction, while the height above the horizon indicated their latitude.

During the day, the Polynesians relied on the sun's position to navigate. They noted the sun's position at sunrise and sunset to determine the east-west direction, and its height at solar noon to estimate their latitude. The changing colors and patterns of the sea also provided valuable cues about their location in relation to nearby islands.

The Polynesians also had an exceptional understanding of ocean currents and wave patterns. They observed the movement of waves and the behavior of marine life to detect underwater currents, which they used to their advantage during their voyages. By understanding the prevailing currents, they could make strategic decisions about their course.

Another crucial navigational tool was the "stick chart." Made from sticks and shells, these charts depicted the complex patterns of ocean swells around islands, allowing navigators to mentally visualize the shapes and orientations of the islands, even when they were not visible on the horizon. The stick charts served as memory aids, helping navigators internalize the layout of the vast ocean.

Polynesian navigation was not just about reading the natural elements but also involved a deep spiritual connection with the sea and the land. Navigators were highly respected and revered individuals in their communities. Their skills were honed through years of training and experience, and they played a crucial role in the success of voyages, whether for exploration, trade, or settlement.

Perhaps one of the most impressive displays of Polynesian navigation was their ability to undertake long-distance voyages and discover new islands. The Polynesians settled in some of the most remote and isolated islands in the Pacific, including Hawaii, New Zealand, and Easter Island. These remarkable feats of exploration demonstrate the courage and navigational prowess of these ancient seafarers.

With the arrival of European explorers, the art of traditional Polynesian navigation declined, as the new technology offered more efficient ways to travel the seas. However, the knowledge and traditions were not completely lost. In recent years, there has been a revival of interest in Polynesian wayfinding, with efforts to preserve and teach these ancient skills to new generations.

Modern navigators, inspired by the wisdom of their ancestors, have embarked on voyages using traditional methods, reviving the art of wayfinding and reaffirming the importance of connecting with nature and the environment.

The ancient Polynesian wayfinding techniques remain a testament to human ingenuity and the power of observation and intuition. They remind us that even in our technologically advanced world, there is still much to learn from the wisdom and skills of those who navigated the vast oceans with nothing but the stars and the wind as their guides. As we delve into the wonders of Polynesian navigation, we gain a deeper appreciation for the courage, knowledge, and profound connection that allowed these ancient seafarers to explore the unknown and find their way across the ocean's expanse.

Languages of French Polynesia: Beyond French and Tahitian

When we think of French Polynesia, the first languages that come to mind are French and Tahitian. While these two languages are indeed prominent in the archipelago, the linguistic landscape of this diverse region is far more intricate and captivating than one might imagine.

French Polynesia is a land of cultural richness, with over 130 islands scattered across the vast Pacific Ocean. Each island has its unique history and heritage, and with that comes a multitude of languages and dialects.

Tahitian is undoubtedly the most widely spoken indigenous language in French Polynesia. It holds a special place in the hearts of the people as the language of their ancestors and their cultural identity. Tahitian is a Polynesian language, part of the larger Austronesian language family, which includes other languages spoken across the Pacific and Southeast Asia.

The French colonization of the islands significantly impacted the linguistic landscape. French became the official language, and it is widely used in government, education, and business. Today, most Polynesians are bilingual, proficient in both Tahitian and French, allowing for seamless communication between the traditional and modern aspects of their lives.

Beyond Tahitian and French, several other languages thrive in French Polynesia. On the island of Rapa, you will encounter the Rapa language, a unique linguistic gem spoken by the local community. On the Marquesas Islands, the locals communicate in Marquesan, which boasts several dialects across the different islands.

In the Tuamotus Archipelago, the inhabitants use Paumotu, a Polynesian language with its own distinct characteristics. In the Austral Islands, the Rapa language is spoken, sharing similarities with other Polynesian tongues while maintaining its individuality.

One of the lesser-known languages is Mangarevan, spoken on the remote island of Mangareva. This language has attracted attention from linguists due to its intriguing complexity and unique features.

It showcases the linguistic diversity found in even the smallest corners of French Polynesia.

Alongside the indigenous languages, French Polynesia is also home to various immigrant communities, each bringing their languages and cultural backgrounds. For instance, on the island of Tahiti, there are significant Chinese and Vietnamese communities whose languages and traditions contribute to the cultural tapestry of the region.

English is also gaining popularity in French Polynesia, particularly in the tourism industry. As the archipelago welcomes visitors from around the world, English serves as a common language for communication and understanding.

Linguistic preservation and revival efforts are ongoing in French Polynesia. Cultural organizations, educational institutions, and community groups work diligently to promote and protect indigenous languages. Language revitalization programs ensure that younger generations have the opportunity to learn and embrace their ancestral tongues.

In recent years, there has been a renewed interest in traditional Polynesian languages. Indigenous languages are celebrated in festivals, song, and dance, strengthening the sense of cultural identity and heritage among the people.

The linguistic diversity of French Polynesia is a reflection of its vibrant history and the resilience of its people. Each language carries the stories, wisdom, and traditions of its community, forming an essential part of the archipelago's collective memory and identity.

Basic Tahitian Language: Useful Phrases for Travelers

As you embark on your journey to French Polynesia, learning some basic Tahitian phrases can enhance your travel experience and help you connect with the warm and welcoming locals. Tahitian is the indigenous language of the islands, and while French is widely spoken, making an effort to use some Tahitian phrases will undoubtedly be appreciated by the people you meet along the way.

1. "Ia ora na" - This is the most common Tahitian greeting, equivalent to saying "Hello" or "Good day."

2. "Mauruuru" - Pronounced "mah-roo-roo," this means "Thank you." A simple "mauruuru" can go a long way in expressing your appreciation.

3. "Nana" - When saying goodbye, use "Nana" to bid farewell.

4. "Aita" - This word means "No" and is useful in everyday conversations.

5. "E" - Pronounced as "ay," it means "Yes."

6. "Māuruuru roa" - Adding "roa" after "mauruuru" makes it a more emphatic "Thank you very much."

7. "Pararii" - If you want to express your delight or admiration for something, say "Pararii" (pronounced "pah-rah-ree").

8. "Fa'aitoito" - This phrase means "Take your time" or "Go slowly," a polite way to encourage someone to not rush.

9. "Haere mai" - When welcoming someone, use "Haere mai," which means "Welcome."

10. "Pāruru" - If you need someone to be quiet or hush, use "Pāruru."

11. "Eaha te huru?" - To ask "What is the price?" when shopping or bargaining.

12. "Pehea te aha?" - When inquiring "How are you?"

13. "Aroha vau ia 'oe" - To express "I love you." (pronounced "ah-roh-hah vow ee-ah oh-ay")

14. "Tama'a maitai" - This phrase means "Bon appétit" and is commonly used before a meal.

15. "Hōtupā'ipai" - When asking for directions, use "Hōtupā'ipai," which means "Can you help me?"

16. "Hōpē" - When indicating the end or finishing something, say "Hōpē."

17. "Oui" - A useful word for travelers, as it means "Yes" in Tahitian.

18. "Non" - For "No," simply say "Non."

19. "I teie mahana" - When referring to "Today."

20. "Aita i teie mahana" - To say "Not today."

By incorporating these basic Tahitian phrases into your conversations, you will undoubtedly leave a positive impression on the local community. The Tahitian people take pride in their language and culture, and by making an effort to use some key phrases, you show respect and appreciation for their heritage.

Tahitians are known for their warm hospitality, and your attempts to speak their language will be met with smiles and encouragement. Even if your pronunciation is not perfect, the effort alone will be appreciated, and you will find that it can open doors to genuine connections and memorable experiences during your stay. As you immerse yourself in the stunning landscapes and vibrant culture of French Polynesia, embracing the Tahitian language adds an extra layer of richness to your journey. Whether you're savoring the delicious local cuisine, exploring the lush rainforests, or lounging on breathtaking beaches, the ability to greet and converse in Tahitian will make your travel encounters even more meaningful and rewarding.

So, don't be shy to give it a try! Embrace the beauty of the Tahitian language and let it be your gateway to a deeper understanding and appreciation of this enchanting corner of the world.

Religion and Spirituality: Ancient and Modern Beliefs

Religion and spirituality have been woven into the fabric of life in French Polynesia since ancient times. The islands are home to a diverse array of belief systems that reflect the cultural richness and spiritual depth of the people.

In ancient Polynesia, before the arrival of European explorers and missionaries, the people practiced a complex and animistic belief system. They revered a pantheon of gods and spirits, each associated with different aspects of nature, such as the sea, the land, and celestial bodies. The gods were believed to have immense power over the elements and played a crucial role in everyday life.

Central to their spiritual practices were rituals and ceremonies performed at sacred places called marae. These marae were stone platforms surrounded by wooden tikis and were used for offerings, prayers, and gatherings. The marae served as places of connection with the divine, where the people sought blessings, guidance, and protection from the gods.

Tahiti's Taputapuātea marae complex is particularly significant and is designated as a UNESCO World Heritage Site. This sprawling site once served as a spiritual and political center, and its importance continues to be acknowledged by the people of French Polynesia today.

With the arrival of European explorers and missionaries, Christianity took root in the islands. Today, Christianity, particularly Protestantism and Catholicism, is the dominant religion in French Polynesia. Churches can be found in nearly every village, and religious practices have become an integral part of daily life for many Polynesians.

Despite the influence of Christianity, traditional beliefs and practices persist in many aspects of Polynesian life. The reverence for nature, the spirits of ancestors, and the gods of the ancient pantheon still lingers, even among those who identify as Christian. This syncretism demonstrates the adaptability and resilience of

Polynesian spirituality, as it evolves and intertwines with new belief systems.

Another fascinating aspect of modern Polynesian spirituality is the concept of mana. Mana is a spiritual force or power believed to reside in people, objects, and natural phenomena. It is associated with authority, influence, and sacredness. The concept of mana holds deep significance in Polynesian culture and is intertwined with the traditional understanding of spirituality.

Traditional art forms, such as dance, music, and carving, are often imbued with spiritual meaning. Dance performances, like the mesmerizing ote'a and aparima, are not merely entertainment but also an expression of cultural identity and a connection to the spiritual world.

The traditional tattoo art of tātau is another practice with deep spiritual meaning. Tattoos are seen as a way to connect with one's ancestors, protect against malevolent forces, and imbue the wearer with mana. The symbols and patterns in tātau tell stories of heritage, identity, and protection.

French Polynesia's spirituality extends to its connection with the natural world. The land and the sea are considered sacred, and the people have a deep respect for the environment and its delicate balance. This spiritual bond with nature underscores the significance of sustainable practices and preservation efforts to protect their beloved islands and ecosystems.

Family and Community: Understanding Social Structure

In French Polynesia, family and community lie at the heart of the cultural fabric, shaping the lives and identities of its people in profound ways. The concept of 'ohana,' or extended family, holds great significance, and it goes beyond biological ties to encompass a broader sense of interconnectedness and mutual support.

In traditional Polynesian society, the family unit extended far beyond the nuclear family. It included parents, children, grandparents, aunts, uncles, and cousins, all living together in close-knit communities. This extended family structure fostered a strong sense of belonging and shared responsibility for one another's well-being.

Elders played a pivotal role in the family and community, serving as the custodians of wisdom, cultural traditions, and ancestral knowledge. Their guidance and teachings were highly valued and passed down through generations, ensuring the continuity of Polynesian heritage.

Respect for one's elders and communal harmony were integral to the social fabric. Polynesians upheld principles of respect, humility, and reciprocity, which strengthened the bond among family members and neighbors.

Today, while urbanization and modernization have led to changes in family dynamics, the essence of 'ohana' remains deeply ingrained in Polynesian culture. Families often live close to one another, and gatherings for special occasions and celebrations are frequent, reinforcing the strong sense of kinship and community.

Another essential aspect of Polynesian social structure is the concept of 'mana' in the family hierarchy. Mana, which also exists in the context of spirituality, refers to the power and authority held by individuals based on their age, wisdom, or social standing. The eldest members of the family typically possess the highest mana and are respected as the leaders and decision-makers.

Gender roles and responsibilities were also well-defined in traditional Polynesian society. Men were often engaged in activities such as fishing, hunting, and warfare, while women played essential roles in food preparation, agriculture, and crafting. However, both genders were valued and contributed significantly to the community's welfare.

Marriage and family life are considered fundamental milestones in Polynesian culture. Weddings are celebrated with joyous festivities, and the union is seen not only as a joining of two individuals but also as a union of their respective families and communities.

Children hold a special place in Polynesian society. They are regarded as gifts from the gods and are cherished by their families and the community. The responsibility of nurturing and educating children is shared among family members, ensuring that the younger generation is instilled with the values and traditions of their heritage.

Polynesians also place great importance on communal activities and gatherings. Festivals, ceremonies, and cultural events are significant occasions for people to come together, celebrate their shared identity, and pass down their customs to future generations. The Heiva festival, for example, is a vibrant celebration of Polynesian culture, featuring traditional dance, music, sports, and craft competitions.

The close-knit sense of community extends beyond family ties to encompass the entire island or village. Villages, known as 'fenua,' function as tightly-knit units, where everyone knows each other and supports one another in times of need. Social gatherings and communal work activities, such as fishing and farming, further reinforce the sense of togetherness and cooperation.

In recent years, as French Polynesia has undergone modernization and globalization, there have been changes in the social structure. However, the core values of family and community continue to be revered and cherished by the Polynesian people.

Tā ne Mahuta and Vā tea: Gods and Mythology

In the enchanting world of Polynesian mythology, the gods Tāne Mahuta and Vātea stand tall as significant figures, each embodying unique attributes and playing pivotal roles in the creation and shaping of the universe.

Tāne Mahuta, often referred to simply as Tāne, is one of the most revered gods in Polynesian mythology. He is the deity of the forests and all living creatures that inhabit them. Tāne is considered the progenitor of humankind and is credited with separating the sky and the earth, creating space for life to flourish in between.

According to the mythological tales, Tāne fashioned the first woman, Hineahuone, from the earth, breathing life into her to populate the world. His creative prowess extended to the natural world, as he gave life to the birds, animals, and plants that grace the islands of French Polynesia.

Tāne Mahuta is often depicted as a tall, handsome figure, symbolizing strength, fertility, and life. The ancient Polynesians revered him, offering prayers and ceremonies in his honor, seeking his blessings for a bountiful harvest, successful voyages, and prosperous endeavors.

Another prominent deity in Polynesian mythology is Vātea, who is closely associated with the sea and the realm of water. Vātea is believed to be the father of gods and men and is often portrayed as a powerful, divine figure ruling over the vast expanse of the ocean.

In the Polynesian creation myth, it is said that Vātea and his wife, Papa, gave birth to the islands and the natural elements that constitute the world. Vātea is considered the creator of the Pacific archipelagoes, including the islands of French Polynesia, and is venerated as the guardian of the seas and all marine life.

The legend of Vātea is interwoven with the spirit of adventure and exploration, as he is said to have embarked on grand voyages across the ocean, navigating through treacherous waters with his divine knowledge and power.

68

Throughout French Polynesia, reverence for Tāne Mahuta and Vātea is evident in various aspects of daily life. From traditional ceremonies to dance performances and artistic expressions, the influence of these gods can be seen in the vibrant culture of the islands.

The ancient mythological stories serve not only as sources of entertainment but also as a means of passing down the history, values, and wisdom of the Polynesian people. Elders and storytellers share these captivating tales with younger generations, ensuring that the rich tapestry of Polynesian mythology remains alive and cherished.

As you traverse the islands of French Polynesia, you will encounter numerous references to Tāne Mahuta and Vātea. Sacred sites, marae, and intricate carvings pay homage to these divine beings, underscoring their enduring significance in the hearts of the Polynesian people.

Visiting these sacred places and learning about the myths and legends surrounding Tāne Mahuta and Vātea offers a deeper understanding of the cultural heritage and spiritual beliefs of the people of French Polynesia.

The legacy of Tāne Mahuta and Vātea endures, not only in the ancient tales but also in the hearts and minds of the Polynesian people who continue to celebrate and honor these gods, finding strength, guidance, and inspiration in the enduring stories of creation and divine intervention.

Tattoos: Indelible Markers of Polynesian Identity

In the tropical paradise of French Polynesia, tattoos are not just an art form; they are a deeply ingrained cultural tradition and a powerful expression of identity. Polynesian tattoos, known as tātau, hold great significance and are more than just decorative body art - they are symbols of heritage, status, and personal stories.

Tātau has a long and storied history in the islands, dating back centuries to ancient Polynesian civilizations. The art of tattooing was passed down through generations, carried forward by skilled tattoo artists known as tufuga ta tatau. These revered craftsmen possessed not only artistic talent but also sacred knowledge of the symbols and designs that held cultural and spiritual meanings.

In traditional Polynesian society, tattoos served as markers of identity, reflecting a person's lineage, rank, and accomplishments. They were often earned through acts of bravery, leadership, or significant life events. Each symbol and pattern told a unique story, creating a visual narrative of a person's journey through life.

The tātau process was not just a physical transformation; it was a deeply spiritual and ritualistic experience. Tattoo sessions were occasions of ceremony and celebration, often accompanied by chanting, prayers, and offerings to the gods. The act of receiving a tattoo was a rite of passage, signifying a person's entrance into adulthood or assuming a new role in the community.

The designs themselves held diverse meanings across different Polynesian cultures. In French Polynesia, specific symbols were associated with the islands' natural elements, such as the ocean, mountains, or flora and fauna. For example, the enata symbol, resembling a human stick figure, represented both the individual and the collective community.

Tātau was not limited to a specific gender; both men and women adorned their bodies with intricate tattoos. Women's tattoos, often placed on the hands, fingers, and lower limbs, were known as puhoro. Men's tattoos, more extensive and covering the torso and limbs, were called pe'a.

The arrival of European explorers in the 18th century brought significant changes to Polynesian societies, including the suppression of traditional practices like tattooing. Christian missionaries viewed tātau as pagan and tried to eradicate the practice, leading to a decline in its prevalence.

However, in recent decades, there has been a resurgence of interest in Polynesian tattoos, driven by a cultural revival and a renewed appreciation for indigenous traditions. Modern tātau artists draw inspiration from traditional designs, infusing them with contemporary interpretations and personalized elements.

Tātau has transcended its traditional role and become a global phenomenon. Many travelers visiting French Polynesia are captivated by the beauty and symbolism of these tattoos and choose to get their own tātau as a memento of their island experiences.

Tattoo studios throughout the islands offer visitors the chance to have their own unique tātau designed and inked by skilled local artists. Each tattoo is carefully crafted, taking into consideration the individual's story, personality, and connection to Polynesian culture.

Beyond the aesthetic appeal, getting a tātau in French Polynesia is a journey of cultural immersion. It provides an opportunity to connect with the rich heritage of the islands, learn about the historical significance of the symbols, and partake in a tradition that has endured for centuries.

Pearl Farming: Exploring the Industry of Black Pearls

In the shimmering waters of French Polynesia lies a fascinating and lucrative industry - pearl farming. This captivating trade revolves around the cultivation of one of the world's most prized gems: the black pearl. These exquisite pearls, also known as Tahitian pearls, have captivated the hearts of jewelry enthusiasts and collectors worldwide, making pearl farming a vital part of the region's economy and cultural heritage.

Pearl farming in French Polynesia traces its roots back to the 1960s when it first emerged as an experimental venture. The black-lipped oyster, Pinctada margaritifera, found in the warm lagoons of the islands, became the focal point of pearl cultivation.

The process of pearl farming is intricate and time-consuming, requiring patience, skill, and a deep understanding of marine ecology. It begins with the collection of oyster spat, or juvenile oysters, which are then carefully nurtured in underwater nurseries. Here, they grow and develop in a controlled environment, shielded from natural predators until they are robust enough to be transferred to the pearl farm.

Once the oysters reach maturity, a tiny nucleus, often a mother-of-pearl bead, is surgically implanted inside the oyster's mantle. This delicate procedure stimulates the oyster's natural defense mechanism, prompting it to secrete layers of nacre, the lustrous substance that forms the pearl. The nucleus acts as the seed around which the pearl gradually forms.

The cultivation process is a delicate balance between art and science. Factors such as water quality, temperature, and the oyster's health play crucial roles in determining the pearl's quality, size, and color. It takes several years for a pearl to develop fully, and during this time, the oysters are closely monitored and cared for by skilled pearl farmers.

Black pearls come in a mesmerizing range of colors, from deep shades of green, blue, and purple to peacock hues with iridescent overtones. The oysters' natural environment influences the pearl's color, making each gem unique and unpredictable.

Once the pearls have matured, they are harvested with great care. Pearl farmers delicately open the oysters, extract the precious pearls, and assess their quality. Pearls that meet the stringent standards are graded and prepared for the market, while those of lower quality are often returned to the farm for further cultivation.

The pearl industry has become an essential pillar of French Polynesia's economy, providing livelihoods for thousands of people across the islands. Pearl farming has not only boosted the region's financial prospects but also contributed to the preservation of the marine ecosystem.

Sustainable pearl farming practices have been implemented to ensure the long-term viability of this industry. Environmental conservation measures, such as maintaining water quality and limiting the number of oysters cultivated, help protect the delicate balance of the lagoons and safeguard the oysters' natural habitats.

The allure of black pearls extends beyond their economic value. These stunning gems hold deep cultural significance for the people of French Polynesia. Pearls are often incorporated into traditional jewelry, worn during important ceremonies, and gifted as symbols of love and respect.

Tourists visiting French Polynesia have the opportunity to learn about pearl farming through guided tours of pearl farms. These tours offer insights into the intricate cultivation process and the dedication of pearl farmers to their craft.

Copra Production: The Essence of Polynesian Economy

In the idyllic archipelago of French Polynesia, copra production stands as a cornerstone of the region's economy, woven into the fabric of daily life and cultural heritage. Derived from the dried meat of coconuts, copra has been a vital commodity for centuries, sustaining livelihoods, supporting communities, and shaping the economic landscape of the islands.

The copra production process begins with the harvesting of ripe coconuts from palm trees that dot the landscapes of the islands. This labor-intensive task is often a communal effort, with families and villages coming together to gather the precious harvest.

Once collected, the coconuts are split open, and the white flesh is carefully removed from the shell. This flesh, known as copra, is then laid out to dry under the sun. The tropical climate of French Polynesia, with its warm temperatures and gentle sea breezes, provides an ideal environment for the copra to dry naturally.

Drying can take several days, during which time the moisture content of the copra is reduced significantly, ensuring its longevity and suitability for processing and export. The dried copra transforms from a soft, white flesh into a firm, brown substance with a distinct coconut aroma.

Traditionally, copra production was a laborious and time-consuming endeavor. Families and communities would engage in manual processing, ensuring that every coconut was meticulously transformed into copra. However, as technology advanced, mechanized methods were introduced to streamline the production process, increasing efficiency and output.

Copra holds immense economic value for French Polynesia. The dried coconut meat is a versatile commodity, serving as a primary ingredient in various products, including coconut oil, soap, cosmetics, and animal feed. Coconut oil, in particular, is highly sought after for its culinary, medicinal, and cosmetic applications, making it a significant export for the region.

In addition to its economic importance, copra production holds cultural significance for the people of French Polynesia. The coconut tree, often referred to as the "Tree of Life," is deeply intertwined with the local way of life, providing sustenance, shelter, and raw materials for a myriad of traditional crafts.

Throughout the islands, copra is celebrated through festivals and cultural events, where the process of harvesting and drying coconuts is showcased and honored. These festivities offer visitors a glimpse into the heart of Polynesian culture, highlighting the profound connection between the people and their natural resources.

As with any industry, copra production also faces challenges and uncertainties. Fluctuating global demand, market prices, and climate change can impact the viability and profitability of copra farming. However, the resilience and ingenuity of the Polynesian people have allowed them to adapt to these challenges and find innovative solutions to sustain their livelihoods.

Impact of Tourism: Balancing Preservation and Development

In the turquoise waters and lush landscapes of French Polynesia, tourism has emerged as a significant force that shapes the islands' economy, culture, and environment. The allure of pristine beaches, vibrant marine life, and the enchanting Polynesian way of life has drawn travelers from around the globe, seeking a taste of paradise. As the tourism industry flourishes, it brings with it both benefits and challenges, necessitating a delicate balance between preserving the islands' natural beauty and fostering sustainable development.

The impact of tourism on French Polynesia has been multifaceted. On one hand, the influx of tourists has injected much-needed revenue into the local economy, contributing to job creation and supporting small businesses. Hotels, restaurants, tour operators, and artisanal shops thrive on the demand from visitors eager to immerse themselves in the island experience.

Moreover, tourism has played a vital role in preserving the cultural heritage of the Polynesian people. Traditional dance performances, music, arts, and crafts have all been revitalized and celebrated, with tourists embracing and supporting these cherished customs.

However, the rapid growth of tourism also poses significant challenges to the delicate ecosystem of the islands. The increasing number of visitors can strain natural resources, disrupt fragile ecosystems, and lead to issues such as overfishing, pollution, and habitat destruction.

French Polynesia is renowned for its vibrant coral reefs, home to a diverse array of marine life. However, excessive tourism-related activities, such as snorkeling, diving, and boating, can put stress on these delicate ecosystems, leading to coral bleaching and degradation.

To counteract these threats, sustainable tourism practices have been adopted. Initiatives to protect marine reserves, promote responsible fishing, and minimize plastic waste are becoming integral components of the tourism industry's efforts to preserve the islands' natural beauty.

Another challenge arising from tourism is the potential impact on traditional culture and ways of life. As the islands become more exposed to outside influences, there is a risk of cultural commodification and dilution. Striking a balance between showcasing the rich cultural heritage and avoiding exploitation is paramount to preserving the essence of Polynesian identity.

The concept of eco-tourism has gained traction as a means of harmonizing tourism with conservation efforts. By encouraging tourists to engage in responsible and sustainable activities that respect the environment and local customs, eco-tourism seeks to promote an authentic and meaningful travel experience.

As the tourism industry continues to evolve, it is essential for policymakers, businesses, and travelers to work hand in hand in safeguarding the delicate balance between preservation and development. The French Polynesian government, along with local communities, has taken significant strides to ensure that tourism's benefits are harnessed responsibly and that the islands' natural and cultural treasures are safeguarded for future generations.

By supporting initiatives that prioritize conservation, respecting local traditions, and minimizing ecological footprints, visitors to French Polynesia can contribute to the islands' sustainable development while relishing the unparalleled beauty and authenticity of this South Pacific paradise.

Challenges of Climate Change: Protecting the Fragile Ecosystem

In the midst of the breathtaking beauty of French Polynesia lies a growing concern that threatens the very essence of this tropical paradise - the impact of climate change. As the global climate continues to shift, the islands of French Polynesia are experiencing a series of challenges that put their delicate ecosystem at risk. Rising sea levels, coral bleaching, extreme weather events, and changing weather patterns are all part of the complex tapestry of climate change effects, which demand urgent attention and collaborative efforts to safeguard the islands' natural wonders.

One of the most pressing challenges faced by French Polynesia is the rise in sea levels. As temperatures increase, polar ice caps melt, causing sea levels to rise globally. This poses a significant threat to low-lying atolls and coastal regions in French Polynesia, putting them at risk of erosion, flooding, and saltwater intrusion into freshwater sources.

Coral reefs, an iconic feature of the islands, are also under severe strain from climate change. Rising ocean temperatures and increased acidity lead to coral bleaching, a phenomenon where corals expel the colorful algae that provide them with essential nutrients. Without these symbiotic algae, the corals lose their vibrant colors and become more susceptible to disease and death. The loss of coral reefs not only impacts marine biodiversity but also jeopardizes the natural barrier that protects the islands from the force of ocean waves.

In addition to coral bleaching, French Polynesia is experiencing more frequent and intense extreme weather events, such as tropical storms and cyclones. These natural disasters can cause widespread damage to infrastructure, disrupt communities, and lead to economic setbacks.

Changing weather patterns also influence rainfall and drought patterns in the islands. Unpredictable weather can affect agriculture, water supply, and overall biodiversity, disrupting the delicate balance of the ecosystems that support life in French Polynesia.

The effects of climate change are not limited to the natural environment; they also have implications for the social and cultural fabric of the islands. Local communities are increasingly vulnerable to the impacts of climate change, from loss of livelihoods in fishing and agriculture to displacement from their ancestral lands due to rising sea levels.

Addressing the challenges of climate change in French Polynesia requires a multi-faceted approach that involves collaboration between the government, local communities, businesses, and international organizations. The French Polynesian government has taken significant steps to mitigate the impacts of climate change and adapt to its effects.

Sustainable practices are being promoted in various sectors, from eco-friendly tourism initiatives to renewable energy projects. The use of solar power, wind energy, and hydroelectricity is gaining momentum, reducing the islands' dependence on fossil fuels and mitigating greenhouse gas emissions.

Conservation efforts to protect and restore coral reefs are also a priority. Marine protected areas and sanctuaries have been established to safeguard marine biodiversity, while coral restoration programs are underway to rebuild damaged reef ecosystems.

Education and awareness play a crucial role in tackling climate change challenges. Environmental organizations and local communities work together to raise awareness about the impacts of climate change and the importance of conservation and sustainable practices.

Art of Outrigger Canoeing: Traditional Sport and Recreation

In the azure waters of French Polynesia, a centuries-old tradition thrives, connecting the people of the islands with their rich maritime heritage - outrigger canoeing. This artful and time-honored sport showcases the skill, strength, and unity of the Polynesian people as they navigate the vast ocean on graceful vessels adorned with outriggers, wooden extensions that provide stability and balance.

Outrigger canoeing is deeply rooted in the culture and history of French Polynesia, dating back to ancient times when the early Polynesians voyaged across the vast Pacific Ocean, exploring and settling new lands. These sturdy canoes, crafted with precision from locally sourced materials, enabled the Polynesians to traverse great distances, relying on the stars, wind, and ocean currents for navigation.

Today, outrigger canoeing remains a beloved pastime, with local communities and visitors alike embracing the sport's traditions and camaraderie. The wooden canoes, now complemented with modern materials, continue to be handcrafted by skilled artisans, who pass down their knowledge from generation to generation.

Outrigger canoeing is not merely a sport; it embodies the essence of Polynesian culture, reflecting the deep connection between the people and the sea. Canoeing competitions and races are celebrated events that bring together communities, fostering a sense of unity, pride, and friendly rivalry.

The sport's cultural significance is often reflected in various traditional ceremonies, where the canoes are blessed and adorned with elaborate decorations. These ceremonies pay homage to the gods and ancestors, seeking their protection and guidance for safe voyages on the open waters.

For those seeking a taste of this time-honored tradition, guided outrigger canoe tours are readily available in French Polynesia. These tours offer a unique opportunity to learn the art of paddling from local experts, who share their knowledge of the ocean, stars, and ancient navigation techniques.

Outrigger canoeing is not limited to competitive racing; it also serves as a recreational activity for individuals and families to explore the beauty of the lagoons and coastlines. The gentle rhythm of paddling in sync with the ocean's flow fosters a deep sense of connection with nature and a profound appreciation for the islands' breathtaking landscapes.

Beyond its cultural and recreational aspects, outrigger canoeing plays a vital role in preserving the islands' marine environment. As paddlers glide through the crystal-clear waters, they bear witness to the fragile beauty of the coral reefs and marine life. This firsthand experience instills a sense of stewardship and responsibility to protect and conserve the precious marine ecosystems.

Outrigger canoeing is a celebration of Polynesian resilience, artistry, and unwavering respect for the natural world. It symbolizes the unity of the people, bridging the gap between generations and keeping the flames of tradition alive.

Land and Water Sports: Thrilling Adventures for All

In the enchanting playground of French Polynesia, adventure awaits both on land and in the shimmering waters. The islands offer a plethora of thrilling sports and activities that cater to all levels of enthusiasts. Whether you seek adrenaline-pumping experiences or a leisurely exploration of nature's wonders, French Polynesia has something to offer everyone.

For those who prefer to keep their feet on solid ground, hiking is a popular choice. The lush landscapes of the islands are adorned with verdant mountains, hidden valleys, and cascading waterfalls, providing a picturesque backdrop for hikers of all levels. Trails vary in difficulty, offering everything from gentle strolls to challenging treks, each offering unique vistas and encounters with the islands' abundant wildlife.

Mountain biking is another land-based activity that allows adventurers to explore the islands' diverse terrains. From rugged dirt trails to scenic coastal routes, bikers can pedal through tropical forests, past vibrant flora, and along pristine beaches. With each turn of the wheel, a new adventure unfolds, offering an immersive experience into the heart of French Polynesia's natural beauty.

For water enthusiasts, the turquoise lagoons and azure ocean waters beckon with an array of thrilling activities. Snorkeling is a must-do for anyone eager to discover the vibrant marine life that thrives beneath the surface. With snorkel and mask in hand, explorers can glide alongside colorful coral reefs, encountering an astonishing variety of tropical fish, rays, and even gentle sharks.

Scuba diving takes underwater exploration to new depths. French Polynesia is renowned for its world-class dive sites, where divers can venture into the mesmerizing blue expanse to encounter majestic manta rays, curious dolphins, and graceful humpback whales during their migratory season. The coral gardens and underwater caves offer an immersive experience into a whole new realm of enchantment.

For those seeking high-speed excitement, jet skiing and parasailing are exhilarating water sports that promise adrenaline rushes and panoramic views of the islands. Zooming across the water's surface or soaring high above, adventurers can witness the stunning landscapes from a unique perspective.

French Polynesia's serene lagoons are also ideal for kayaking and paddleboarding. Paddlers can leisurely glide through calm waters, taking in the peaceful surroundings and enjoying close encounters with the friendly marine life that often ventures near the shoreline.

In addition to these individual sports, French Polynesia offers opportunities for team-based activities. Beach volleyball and beach soccer are popular choices, allowing friends and families to bond and compete in the soft, sandy shores.

French Polynesia's diverse landscapes also provide the perfect backdrop for rock climbing and canyoning adventures. Experienced climbers can ascend the rugged cliffs, while canyoning enthusiasts can navigate through lush valleys and cascading waterfalls, guided by expert local instructors.

As with any adventure sport, safety is paramount. Tour operators and adventure companies in French Polynesia prioritize the well-being of participants, providing expert guides and top-notch equipment to ensure a safe and enjoyable experience.

No matter your age or level of experience, French Polynesia's land and water sports offer an extraordinary range of activities for everyone to relish. Whether you seek to challenge your limits, connect with nature, or simply have fun in this tropical paradise, the islands' vibrant and diverse offerings promise thrilling adventures that will create lasting memories of a lifetime. So dive in, paddle out, and step into the wild wonderland of French Polynesia's land and water sports.

Island Hopping: Creating Your Ideal Itinerary

Embarking on an island-hopping adventure in French Polynesia promises an unforgettable journey through the South Pacific's most exquisite gems. With 118 islands scattered across five archipelagos, each possessing its distinct charm and allure, crafting your ideal itinerary becomes an exciting and personalized endeavor.

The Society Islands, home to the iconic islands of Tahiti, Moorea, Bora Bora, and Huahine, are an ideal starting point for many travelers. Tahiti, the largest and most populous island, serves as the gateway to French Polynesia, offering international flights and a vibrant blend of city life and natural beauty. A visit to the lush and mountainous island of Moorea, just a short ferry ride away, unveils captivating landscapes and a tranquil atmosphere.

No trip to French Polynesia is complete without a stop at Bora Bora, renowned for its luxurious overwater bungalows, turquoise lagoon, and mesmerizing Mount Otemanu. Huahine, often referred to as the "Garden of Eden," exudes an untouched charm, with its lush forests, pristine beaches, and ancient archaeological sites.

For those seeking a more remote and secluded experience, the Tuamotus archipelago offers a stunning collection of atolls, including Rangiroa and Fakarava. These tranquil paradise isles are a haven for divers and snorkelers, showcasing vibrant coral reefs and abundant marine life.

The Marquesas Islands, with their rugged beauty and lush landscapes, are a true explorer's paradise. Nuku Hiva and Hiva Oa, home to impressive cliffs, dramatic waterfalls, and intriguing ancient ruins, offer an authentic and off-the-beaten-path adventure.

The Australs and the Gambier archipelago, less frequented by tourists, provide an opportunity for a deeper immersion into Polynesian culture and traditions. Rurutu and Tubuai, part of the Australs, are known for their unique landscapes and vibrant culture, while Mangareva in the Gambiers boasts captivating lagoons and historical sites.

The Tuamotus, Marquesas, Australs, and Gambier islands are often accessed by inter-island flights, making island-hopping convenient and accessible. However, some atolls can only be reached by cargo ships or passenger cruise ships, adding an adventurous twist to your journey.

Crafting your ideal itinerary is all about striking a balance between relaxation, exploration, and cultural immersion. Whether you envision a luxurious retreat in a lavish resort, an adrenaline-pumping water sports extravaganza, or a soulful journey to uncover ancient legends and traditions, French Polynesia caters to every desire.

While planning your island-hopping adventure, it's essential to consider the best time to visit each region. The dry season, from May to October, is often favored for its pleasant weather and lower humidity. However, each season holds its unique appeal, and the tropical climate ensures warm temperatures throughout the year.

To optimize your travel experience, seek advice from experienced travel agents or tour operators specializing in French Polynesia. They can help tailor your itinerary to match your interests and preferences, ensuring you make the most of your time in this captivating corner of the world.

As you hop from island to island, take the opportunity to savor the local cuisine, engage with warm-hearted locals, and immerse yourself in the vibrant arts and customs. Be open to serendipitous encounters and breathtaking surprises that this archipelagic wonderland has to offer.

Planning Your Trip: Tips and Essentials for Travelers

Congratulations on choosing French Polynesia as your next travel destination! Your upcoming journey to this tropical paradise is bound to be filled with enchantment, adventure, and unforgettable experiences. As you prepare for your trip, here are some essential tips and information to ensure a smooth and enjoyable travel experience.

1. Travel Documents: Ensure that you have a valid passport with at least six months' validity from your departure date. For most travelers, a visa is not required for stays of up to 90 days. However, it's always best to check the entry requirements based on your nationality.

2. Best Time to Visit: French Polynesia enjoys a warm and tropical climate year-round. The dry season, from May to October, is generally considered the best time to visit, offering pleasant weather and lower humidity. The wet season, from November to April, brings occasional rain showers and higher humidity, but also lush greenery and fewer crowds.

3. Booking Flights and Accommodations: Plan your trip in advance and book your flights and accommodations early to secure the best rates and availability. French Polynesia's main international gateway is Faa'a International Airport in Papeete, Tahiti.

4. Packing Essentials: Pack light and smart for your island adventure. Don't forget to include essentials like sunscreen, insect repellent, a wide-brimmed hat, sunglasses, comfortable clothing, swimwear, and sturdy walking shoes for exploring.

5. Health Precautions: Visit your healthcare provider well before your trip to ensure you are up-to-date on vaccinations and receive any necessary travel-specific health advice. Mosquito-borne illnesses, such as dengue fever, are present in some regions, so take precautions accordingly.

6. Currency and Money Matters: The local currency is the French Pacific franc (XPF). Although credit cards are widely accepted in major establishments, it's advisable to carry some cash for smaller purchases and local markets.

7. Language: French and Tahitian are the official languages, but English is spoken in most tourist areas. Learning a few basic Tahitian phrases can be a fun and respectful way to engage with the local culture.

8. Cultural Etiquette: Polynesian culture places great importance on respect and courtesy. When visiting villages or sacred sites, it's essential to be mindful of local customs and traditions.

9. Island-Hopping: If you plan to visit multiple islands, consider booking inter-island flights or cruise packages in advance to optimize your travel time and experience the diverse beauty of French Polynesia.

10. Respect for the Environment: The pristine natural beauty of French Polynesia is fragile and deserves preservation. When exploring the islands, practice responsible tourism by avoiding damage to coral reefs and ecosystems and properly disposing of waste.

11. Travel Insurance: Ensure you have comprehensive travel insurance that covers medical emergencies, trip cancellations, and unexpected incidents.

12. Time Zone: French Polynesia operates on Tahiti Time (GMT-10), which may vary from your home country. Adjust your schedules accordingly to make the most of your days in paradise.

13. Connectivity: While French Polynesia offers modern amenities and connectivity, keep in mind that some remote areas may have limited internet access.

14. Local Transportation: Taxis, buses, and rental cars are available on most islands, making it convenient to explore at your own pace.

15. Immerse in the Culture: Embrace the warm hospitality of the local people, attend cultural events, and participate in

traditional activities to create lasting memories and meaningful connections.

With these essential tips, you are well on your way to creating the perfect itinerary for your dream trip to French Polynesia. Be prepared for an immersive experience in a world of natural wonders, cultural riches, and warm Polynesian hospitality. Get ready to embark on an adventure of a lifetime as you uncover the magic of the South Pacific and create memories that will stay with you forever. Bon voyage!

Cultural Sensitivity: Respecting Local Traditions

As you venture into the captivating world of French Polynesia, you will find yourself immersed in a rich tapestry of culture and traditions that have been passed down through generations. Embracing and respecting these customs is not only an essential aspect of responsible travel but also a gateway to a more meaningful and authentic experience. Cultural sensitivity is the key to fostering a genuine connection with the local people and understanding the heart and soul of this enchanting destination.

1. Greetings and Respect: Polynesians place great importance on greetings and respect. When meeting someone, a warm smile and a friendly "ia ora na" or "mauruuru" (hello and thank you) go a long way in showing your appreciation for their culture.

2. Dress Code: In more traditional settings and villages, modest attire is encouraged. Cover your shoulders and knees when visiting sacred sites or participating in cultural events as a sign of respect.

3. Removing Shoes: It is customary to remove your shoes before entering someone's home or a sacred space. This practice symbolizes leaving outside impurities and entering with a pure heart.

4. Accepting Gifts: If someone offers you a gift or invites you into their home, graciously accept it as a gesture of goodwill. Gifts may be simple, but they carry great meaning in Polynesian culture.

5. Treading Lightly: The islands' delicate ecosystems are deeply cherished by the local people. Practice responsible tourism by avoiding littering, disturbing wildlife, or damaging coral reefs.

6. Sacred Sites: Many areas in French Polynesia hold cultural and spiritual significance. When visiting marae (ancient temples) or other sacred sites, follow any rules or restrictions in place and approach with reverence.

7. Photography and Videography: Always ask for permission before taking photos or videos of local people or their

homes. Some individuals may be uncomfortable with being photographed, especially during private moments.

8. Language: Learning a few basic Tahitian phrases is not only helpful for communication but also appreciated by the local community. Efforts to speak the local language are often met with warmth and smiles.

9. Etiquette in Markets: When shopping at local markets, engage with vendors respectfully and avoid haggling too aggressively. Polynesian markets are vibrant and colorful, offering a unique glimpse into daily life.

10. Traditional Performances: Dance and music are integral parts of Polynesian culture. When attending cultural performances, be an attentive and respectful audience, and refrain from inappropriate behavior.

11. Traditional Art and Crafts: Handcrafted items carry deep cultural significance. Support local artisans by purchasing authentic products, understanding the stories behind them, and avoiding counterfeit goods.

12. Family and Community: Polynesian society places strong emphasis on family bonds and community ties. Show interest in learning about their family structure and customs, as it reveals the heart of their cultural identity.

13. Time and Pace: Embrace the concept of "island time," where life unfolds at a leisurely pace. Allow yourself to relax, savor the moment, and enjoy the unhurried rhythm of the islands.

14. Sacred Objects: If you encounter traditional objects or artifacts, treat them with respect and avoid touching or disturbing them. These items may hold spiritual significance or cultural heritage.

15. Celebrate Local Festivals: Participating in local festivals and events offers a glimpse into the heart of Polynesian traditions. Enjoy the lively music, dance, and feasting, and celebrate alongside the locals.

By being culturally sensitive and open-minded, you open yourself to an authentic connection with the people of French Polynesia. Your willingness to respect and embrace their traditions will be met

—

with genuine warmth and hospitality. In return, you will gain a deeper appreciation for this beautiful land and its people, forging memories and experiences that will remain etched in your heart forever.

French Polynesia's Future: Embracing Sustainability and Growth

As French Polynesia continues to enchant travelers with its pristine beauty and vibrant culture, the archipelago faces the challenge of balancing tourism-driven growth with the preservation of its fragile ecosystems and cultural heritage. Embracing sustainability is vital for the future of this paradise, ensuring that its unique wonders remain intact for generations to come.

1. Protecting Marine Biodiversity: The stunning coral reefs and abundant marine life of French Polynesia are essential to its allure. Conservation efforts, including marine protected areas and sustainable fishing practices, are crucial to safeguard these delicate ecosystems.

2. Climate Change Mitigation: Like many island nations, French Polynesia is vulnerable to the impacts of climate change, including rising sea levels and extreme weather events. The government is actively engaged in international climate agreements and sustainable initiatives to reduce carbon emissions and address these challenges.

3. Renewable Energy: To reduce reliance on imported fossil fuels and promote sustainability, French Polynesia has been investing in renewable energy sources such as solar, wind, and hydropower. These efforts contribute to a greener and more self-sufficient future.

4. Waste Management: With the increase in tourism, managing waste becomes a pressing issue. The government and local communities are working together to implement recycling programs, reduce single-use plastics, and promote responsible waste disposal.

5. Sustainable Tourism: The tourism industry plays a significant role in the economy of French Polynesia, but sustainable tourism practices are vital to protect the natural and cultural assets of the islands. Eco-friendly accommodations, responsible tour operators, and

---

education on sustainable travel are essential aspects of this endeavor.

6. Balancing Development and Preservation: Preserving the traditional way of life and cultural heritage while embracing economic growth is a delicate balance. Responsible development ensures that infrastructure and tourism activities align with environmental and cultural conservation.

7. Biodiversity Conservation: French Polynesia is home to unique plant and animal species found nowhere else on Earth. Conservation efforts, including the protection of endemic species and their habitats, are essential to maintain this rich biodiversity.

8. Traditional Knowledge: Embracing traditional knowledge and practices is an integral part of sustainability. Local communities often hold valuable insights into sustainable agriculture, fishing methods, and natural resource management.

9. Education and Awareness: Raising awareness among residents and tourists alike about the importance of sustainability fosters a collective responsibility for preserving French Polynesia's treasures. Educational programs, workshops, and eco-tourism initiatives are contributing to this awareness.

10. Supporting Local Economies: Encouraging visitors to purchase locally made products, support small businesses, and engage in cultural exchanges contributes to the economic well-being of local communities.

11. Preserving Indigenous Languages: While French is the official language, preserving and promoting indigenous languages, such as Tahitian, remains crucial to preserving cultural identity and heritage.

12. Responsible Tourism Practices: Travelers can actively participate in sustainability efforts by choosing eco-conscious accommodations, respecting local customs, and supporting eco-friendly activities.

13. Ecological Research: Collaborative efforts between scientists, local communities, and the government are essential for ongoing ecological research to better understand and protect the unique ecosystems of the islands.

14. Partnerships and Collaborations: Engaging in partnerships with international organizations, neighboring countries, and other island nations fosters knowledge sharing and mutual support in addressing shared environmental challenges.

By proactively embracing sustainability, French Polynesia is forging a path towards a resilient and thriving future. The commitment to preserving its natural wonders and cultural treasures is not just a responsibility of the local community and the government, but also of every visitor who falls under the spell of its beauty. Together, we can protect and nurture the splendor of French Polynesia for generations to come, ensuring that this paradise remains a symbol of harmony between nature and culture in the heart of the Pacific Ocean.

Epilogue

As we come to the end of our journey through the enchanting world of French Polynesia, we reflect on the wonders we have discovered and the experiences we have embraced. From the turquoise waters and powder-white beaches to the vibrant culture and warm hospitality, this South Pacific paradise has left an indelible mark on our hearts and souls.

French Polynesia's allure lies not only in its breathtaking landscapes but also in the resilience of its people and their dedication to preserving their cultural heritage and natural treasures. Through the chapters of this book, we have delved into the depths of its history, the richness of its traditions, and the splendor of its wildlife.

We have traced the footsteps of the early Polynesian settlers, the arrival of European explorers, and the subsequent waves of influence that shaped the islands' history. We have marveled at the diversity of marine life, from humpback whales and dolphins to the kaleidoscope of colors found in its coral reefs.

The tantalizing flavors of Tahitian cuisine have delighted our palates, and the traditional arts and crafts have captivated our imaginations. We have witnessed the passion and rhythm of Polynesian music and dance, felt the heartbeat of their spirituality, and explored the meaning behind ancient symbols and mythology.

As we journeyed through the islands, we learned to navigate with the wisdom of ancient wayfinders, respecting the customs and traditions of the local communities we encountered. We celebrated the unity and strength of family and community, and we marveled at the tales of gods and deities woven into the fabric of Polynesian culture.

In the wake of our exploration, we also recognized the challenges and responsibilities that lie ahead for French Polynesia. Balancing the delicate harmony between tourism, sustainability, and cultural preservation remains a pressing priority for the islands.

As we bid farewell to this paradise, let us carry with us the lessons of cultural sensitivity, environmental stewardship, and the appreciation for the interconnectedness of all living beings. Our encounters with French Polynesia have left us with a profound appreciation for the beauty and resilience of nature and the enduring power of tradition and heritage.

May the enchantment of French Polynesia continue to inspire and educate travelers from all corners of the globe. As we return to our daily lives, let us remember the magic of this tropical haven and the responsibility we hold to protect and preserve it for future generations.

In closing, let us take with us the spirit of aloha and mauruuru (thank you) to the people of French Polynesia, who have welcomed us with open arms and shared the beauty of their home. May their culture and land forever thrive, and may our memories of this paradise remain etched in our hearts as a reminder of the wonders that exist in this world.

Until we meet again, may the spirit of French Polynesia continue to guide our journeys and remind us to embrace the treasures of every destination with humility, gratitude, and reverence.

Mauruuru roa, French Polynesia, for an unforgettable adventure and the gift of inspiration that will stay with us for a lifetime. Farewell, until we meet again in the embrace of your turquoise waters and golden sunsets.